The Death
of a
Parent

The Death
of a
Parent

*Reflections for Adults Mourning the Loss
of a Father or Mother*

Delle Chatman

Meditations by Rev. William Kenneally

ACTA
ASSISTING CHRISTIANS TO ACT
PUBLICATIONS

The Death of a Parent
Reflections for Adults Mourning the Loss of a Father or Mother
by Delle Chatman
with meditations by Rev. William Kenneally

Edited by Gregory F. Augustine Pierce
Cover design by Tom A. Wright
Cover photo by Delle Chatman
Typesetting by Desktop Edit Shop, Inc.

Published by: ACTA Publications
               Assisting Christians To Act
               5559 W. Howard St.
               Skokie, IL 60077
               800-397-2282

Library of Congress Catalog Number: 2001089151

ISBN: 0-87946-224-8

Printed in the United States of America

Year: 10 09 08
Printing: 10 9 8 7 6 5 4

Contents

To my parents
James Icelius Chatman, Sr. and Joyce Chatman
and
My grandmother, Aloia Adams
Wonderful pillars of faith, all three!
Godspeed!

Introduction
The Test of Faith

I hate the title of this book.

I hate the book's title because I hate being qualified twice over to write on this subject. I hate the title because it says in big bold print what I resist saying out loud, even though I buried the second of my parents over two years ago. As if watching my twin titans die weren't enough of a gut-wrenching reminder of my own mortality, I myself am a parent. So along side the grim vision of my own inevitable, inescapable passing from this plane of existence, I see my daughter, who is now only five, having to deal with that loss one day. I don't like to think about Ramona having to face pain of any kind, and especially not the searing wound of losing the mother and father I know she loves.

The truth is, she and I have already discussed death at great length, especially what would happen to her should "something happen" to me.

We were walking from her pre-school to the bakery for a treat one day. I was hoping a cookie might buy me an extra helping of her patience so I could make a few more stops, run a few more errands before dinner time. It's a hop, skip and a jump down a residential block from Ramona's schoolhouse to the health food restaurant's tiny bakery, so we hoofed it, hand in hand.

When I walk with her, I usually stroll on the street-side of the sidewalk for safety's sake, like gentlemen sometimes do for ladies—even in this politically correct 21st century. For some reason, this particular afternoon Ramona asked me why it was better that I be the one walking close to the street. Up until that afternoon, she had accepted that arrangement as one of the many unspoken rules adults delighted in inflicting upon their children. But apparently, at what seemed to me a surprisingly early age, her tolerance for unquestioned edicts had evaporated. She demanded to know "Why?"

"Because if you decided to run out into the street for some reason, I could stop you."

"I'm not going to run out into the street, Mommy," she said, rolling her eyes. "I'm six years old now, you know."

"Yes, I know, but you might see something interesting over *near* the street," I said, trying to give her credit for advancing maturity. "You might forget all about the cars or trip and fall over the curb or something. "

She was silent for a moment, but her face said that there had to be more to it than that, and of course there was.

"Well, also," I confessed, "Mommy walks on the street-side of the sidewalk because if someone accidentally lost control of their car and ran up on the curb I could push you out of the way easier than you could push me out of the way."

"But then the car would hit *you*."

"I could move out of the way faster than you."

"I can run faster than you can, Mommy."

"I know," I said, thinking *you cheeky little girl* under my breath. "But I pay more attention to what's going on around me than you do. I'd probably see a car coming sooner than you would."

"But why is it better for you to get hit than for me to get hit?"

I must have moaned out loud, because she tugged on my hand a little harder than usual. She knew she'd struck gold: a deep truth was lurking somewhere, she could smell it.

"I'm bigger than you," I fumbled. "The car might not hurt me as much as it would hurt you."

I was on the run, for sure.

Ramona frowned. "We're talking about a car, Mom. A car can kill you, too, you know. You said…" and she recited back at me some grave warning I'd used to scare her away from the street.

I'd evidently done almost too good a job of terrifying her, too, because I remembered that she'd had a nightmare about a little boy being hit shortly after my "don't run into the street" lecture. The dream haunted her for days. Now I had made her envision me all a-squish in the road.

Desperate to close the subject, I threw subtlety to the wind. "Well, better that a car would kill me than you," I said.

"Why?" she wailed.

Why, oh, why do they always ask why?

"Because I've lived a long, long time already, Ramona, and you have a whole lifetime ahead of you."

"But what happens to me if you die?"

I took a deep breath and tried to use the most casual tone of voice possible to describe who would care for her if "something happened" to me. One instinctively dodges the word "death" when talking about it to kids, but the subterfuge is futile. Eventually, they squeeze the truth out of you.

As well they should.

Another mini-silence slipped by while Ramona weighed the emotional consequences of moving in with her father and his new wife. That sat pretty well with her actually, which made me breathe a little easier about that heretofore unmentioned contingency plan. Good. I could make it part of my trust or will or whatever it was I need to write to make sure my posthumous desires for her care were met. But then Ramona needed to know who would take care of her if something happened to her dad. I said her godmother would take her in. And then what if something happened to her godmother? Well then maybe she'd like to live with her stepmom, and that was okay. But what if something happened to her stepmom?

"I don't think God would put you through all that, Ramona."

She seemed to accept that dodge. She has a healthy nugget of trust in God's love for her already, thank goodness. I checked to see how close we were to the bakery. A short block's stroll had turned into a marathon.

"I still don't see how it's better for you to die before me," she said finally.

"Because," I said pushing through the bakery door into the comfort of butter-cinnamon smells, "if you died first, it would kill me."

I hate the title of this book.

I hate that there is no one left for me to torture with my whys.

I hate that there is no one left to walk on the street-side of life

11

and be my loving buffer against its hard knocks and the inevitability of my own demise. I hate the title of this book because the experience it describes in its five little words are at once too accurate and too opaque to describe one of the most profound experiences of anyone's lifetime. I hate the title of this book because it forces me to face the reality my six year old knew instinctively somehow awaits her one day.

For soon after we realize that we and our mothers do not occupy one and the same body, we then discover that our parents—both of them together or one by one—can be lost. Sometimes we lose them temporarily in the candy aisle of the grocery store or over by the frozen yogurt shop in the mall. But eventually those guardians to whom our lives were entrusted at the outset leave this earth altogether, and then we—no matter how young or old we are at the time—have to wonder what stands between us and the often awesome, sometimes dangerous, always unpredictable unknowns of life.

And why *is* it better that we lose our guardians before they lose us?

It doesn't feel like anything you would ever have described as "better" or preferable. It feels more like a stiff wind ripping the roof off of your home and leaving you forever exposed to the sky's whims.

Through this book I hope you will track my lurching journey through the emotions and experiences that accompanied the deaths of my mother and father. My double-loss may be your gain. At least I hope will be. For each of my losses was different, just as each and every parent is different. The circumstances of each parent's death—the supporting players, the personalities of the deceased and those left behind, the aftermath, the size and shape of the hole each departure leaves in our hearts, the involuntary changes in the woven tapestry of our lives are all vastly different.

That's why I have chosen the vehicle of fiction to explore this experience. I don't want this book to be about the death of my parents. I want it to be a reflection upon the death of all our parents. Creating a collection of short stories about adults who have suffered this loss made it possible for me to write about what is universal about this transition. I could explore the tiniest details, the seldom anticipated issues that often catch us by surprise, and the broad strokes of change we can see coming but often underestimate.

That, too, is why I've asked my pastor, Father Bill Kenneally, to write a short pastoral meditation at the end of each chapter. Hopefully, his perspective will provide another tier of understanding and consolation.

Before I write anything else, though, let me tell you what the common denominator is between the dual tragedies I've suffered. It's the reason why I can write this book at all. It's the reason why the book may help you right now where you're hurting. It's the one thing that makes this title bearable at all. It's faith.

Both of my parents were Christians whose strong faith grew mighty as the end approached. They both died of lung cancer and saw death on the horizon stalking them. They each had three years to prepare themselves for the end. For a host of reasons, that preparation took a vastly different shape for each of them. They were not married when they died, so they were surrounded by different casts of characters, different levels of material comfort, different entertainments, different instruments of distraction. They had enjoyed different degrees of inner peace and personal satisfaction. They had achieved different levels of intimacy with their children and their friends. They did not have the same will nor the same financial means with which to wage a medical battle for their lives.

But when it was clear the war would be lost no matter what, they both grabbed hold of the same Truth and held on through the very end.

Just as their deaths tested their faith, it also tested mine. Nothing forces you to redefine your existence, to quantify your own values, to assess your own past, present and future, or to trust in God quite like "The Death of a Parent."

Mom died in February of 1994. Dad died in January of 1998. Echoes of their exits still sound loud and clear at times, bringing fresh life-questions before me: some true-or-false, some multiple-choice, some fill-in-the-blank, and many, many essay questions.

I still want to pick up the phone and call them when life throws me a curve. I want to hear them say they're proud of me when I have a breakthrough of some sort. I want to hear their laughter, their voices. I long for the way each of them said my name. I want them to see their granddaughter's latest crayon masterpiece. I want them to hear how well she reads. I want them to experience her incredible beauty. I even want them to continue vexing me with their weaknesses and annoying me with their pet peeves.

You may not want to know this, but I have to write it again: Nothing tests you quite like the death of a parent, and the testing never ends. It's like Ramona's six-year-old wail of "Why?" I kid myself that one day she'll outgrow it, but deep down I know she won't. That why-wail of hers will merely change into a less naked, more insistent demand for profoundly elusive explanations. In much the same way, I don't think we ever get over the death of our parents. We never outgrow it, or outdistance the grief completely. The loss of a mother or father continue to bring to mind a fresh set of truths that need sifting, a new batch of old memories to treasure or trash, a deeper appreciation for wisdom once spurned, new tests of faith custom-made just for the child—no matter what age.

My parents left me a legacy of true faith. It is this "evidence of things unseen" that makes the loss of them bearable and the writing of this book with the horrible title healing. The faith they showed me as they lay dying taught me that now—as I walk my life path without them—I have God holding my hand, strolling on the street-side, guiding and protecting me, having already proven His willingness to die so that I might live.

Taking Care
and Letting Go

From the day we are born, there is a goodbye waiting to be said.

One day, we will know for sure that Daddy won't be coming home from work. Sooner or later, there is a "Mommy has to go now" that cannot be begged away. No matter how old we are at the time, no matter how old our *parents* are, their exit from this world will seem a little unreal and even somehow unfair. Whether we like it or not, there will come an abrupt and unalterable end to the earliest relationship of our lives.

Sometimes death's slow approach insists that decisions must be made, doctors must be consulted, treatments must be embraced or rejected, hands must be held. When the end takes its time arriving, there are often pills and injections to administer, ice cubes to press against dry lips, glassy eyes to close. Those who sit bedside through a death vigil usher their beloved to heaven's gates.

This is sacred ground.

But death does not always give us a "Heads up!" Not every son or daughter is called upon to nurse a dying parent. Sometimes death marches into a family like a crude and raucous party crasher, emboldened by inevitability. Suddenly our lives are changed and will never be the same again.

Whether one is caretaker, witness, or the stricken recipient of a phone call that couldn't be put on hold—the death of a parent tests our ability to handle surprise, helplessness and loss. Whether the end comes quickly or the curtain is drawn slowly over weeks, months or years, we can't help but hope that peace and love will reign in every heart.

And that we will be able to both take good care…and gently let go.

WHEN THEY JUST UP AND DIE
Eric's Story

The afternoon felt California perfect, even though it was a messy Michigan morning in early spring. The cell phone in his golf bag had rung the first time way back on the fifteenth's dogleg and chirped up again on the sixteenth just as he pitched out of the rough at the edge of green. Eric ignored it. Let whoever they were leave a message. He'd call back when he was King of the Fairway, comfortably enthroned in the nineteenth hole clubhouse.

For once, the putts were dropping easy. That dip into the rough on the sixteenth? Just a whisper of trouble on an afternoon of pure bliss. Good thing his kid brother was there, too, hacking his way around the course with him. Eric needed a witness. The usual golf gang would never believe he'd already shaved five strokes off his personal best. His brother triple putted the seventeenth, double-bogeying miserably, and blamed it on the third six-pack of rings that erupted from Eric's bag.

"You gonna get that?" his brother complained.

"Nope," Eric said, lining up his putt. "I'm going to birdie this hole."

The phone fell silent once again.

Eric sank his fifteen footer, pumping his arm and hissing "Yes!" at the sky. He raced at the cup, lifted the dimpled ball to his lips for a kiss, and turned his attention to the eighteenth hole. As he yanked his cart toward the next set of white tees, the phone purred another electronic summons at him.

Uh-uh. No way he was going to let his wife's grocery list omissions preempt the Tiger-Woods-in-a-sudden-death-play-off fantasy he was spinning.

"Come on, Eric," his brother whined. "Answer the phone."

"*You* answer it," Eric said, deciding to let his driver—"Big

Dog"—have at the Par 4 hole. He loved that club. All the woods, really. He loved their length and that warm knob of wood, smooth and elegant, at the end of all that shiny strength. So what if no one used them anymore? So what if titanium was all the rage and Tiger blasted golf into another galaxy using all those space age metals? Woods had been good enough for Eric's dad, the family's first golf fanatic. The dull clack and clank of those old clubs in Eric's brand new golf bag lent him another generation of confidence. Tradition was serving him just fine this afternoon. *Thanks, Dad*, he thought, and polished a grass stain off the driver with his thumb.

"He's not available at the moment," his brother said into the cellphone with a sarcastic pout in his voice. "Can I take a message?"

Eric took a practice swing and addressed the ball.

"This is his brother. Who's this?"

"Easy does it, Eric, my boy," Eric said out loud to himself. "You are more than up to this. Today you *are* golf."

His shoulders led the perfect backswing, his arms followed, smooth as glass.

At the top of the swing, his brother half-groaned, half-growled "What?" into the cellular. A shiver shot up Eric's spine. He pulled the shot, and the ball sailed straight for the trees lining the left rough. He thumped his club's foot down hard against the grass and whirled round to let baby brother have what-for.

But he found the younger man sitting cross-legged on the ground next to Eric's golf bag with the cell phone at his ear, his eyes full of tears. "What?" his brother breathed into the phone again, only softer this time, like a prayer. "But she was *fine*."

One week and a hundred decisions later, Eric helped his father out of the black limousine, guided him over rain-softened grass, and eased him into a seat beside the casket that held the mother of two sons. They were all still in shock, Eric no less than the others. Even so, his usually self-reliant father had depended on his oldest son to navigate their trek through the logistics of loss. Finally sitting down at the graveside, Eric's mind wandered a bit while the priest recited the last scriptural send-off. The golfer in him began studying the grass around the edges of the burial site—beyond the chairs filled with family, beyond the black-cloaked silhouettes of sad-faced friends.

Eric could tell the cemetery had talented groundskeepers. Who nurses this lawn into such cheerful heartiness, he wondered. Couldn't be easy either, keeping it all looking so green and neat. How ever did they trim around all the headstones?

His father's fresh sobs dragged Eric back into the here-and-now. He put his arm around the old man, and concentrated on "Dust to dust. Ashes to ashes."

That's when he realized why he'd chosen that particular casket.

Same warm wood. Same dark grain as his prized Number One driver.

"Big Dog," he whispered, as tears finally shook themselves loose.

PRAYING FOR THEM TO LIVE, PRAYING FOR THEM TO DIE
Felicia's Story

She kicked the treadmill up half a point, and then another half point.

Felicia had promised her father that she'd love herself back into shape if he'd just kick back at the cancer one more time. If he'd beat it one more time, she'd "beat her body under" and reclaim her pre-baby silhouette. If he'd hang on until she returned home at Christmas, she'd show him the svelte daughter of his dreams. Felicia couldn't make it back to that post-college featherweight trim again. That was history. But if he'd climb on top of the chemo-bronco one more time, she'd lift weights and spurn her cheesecake addiction, and they would both be struttin' again by Christmas.

If he'd only....

But he couldn't.

He just couldn't.

All his seventy years began to look and feel like ninety.

All the treatment became punishment.

All his struggling to live only hastened the dying.

The battle had been bravely fought and lost. He was ready to surrender.

Felicia jacked the stair master up two points and let the tears mingle with the sweat. No one noticed. After all, no pain, no gain, right? As long as she kept on stepping, she could cry a river right there in the middle of the health club and pass her frown off as the quintessential pain necessary for that all important gain.

Her father couldn't even talk on the phone anymore, but her mother said he listened to Felicia's calls with fierce attention. Losing his voice was another landmark loss, more cruel than the others. No one loved to talk more than he did. He loved the sound of

19

his own voice. He dominated every conversation. After awhile it would get on people's nerves, even though he often had the most profound things to say. During his disease-imposed silence, Felicia began recalling his words of wisdom and lobbing them back at him so he'd know she had been listening and paying attention.

When she had visited him at Thanksgiving, they both sensed it was the last time.

"Keep it up," he whispered to her in a cracked rasp, and Felicia knew he meant more than the exercise. He meant the discipline and self-love that drove the exercise, fueled her intensified prayer-life and motivated her fresh wave of professional evolution.

"I'll always be with you," he said. "I'll never leave you."

She had hugged him gently, though she wanted to squeeze him tight. Looking back over her shoulder as she left his room, she thought to herself: *This is the last time. This is the last time. This is the last time.*

And from that day on, Felicia worked out harder. She wept away another five pounds. And with every stroke of the stationary bike pedal, she cried: "Please don't let him suffer anymore. Take him, Lord. He's ready. He's waiting. You're the only One who can help him now."

Meditation

The call comes—sometimes from the hospital, sometimes from the funeral director, sometimes from the loving ones at home who go to the telephone directly from the side of the deathbed. It is never routine. Often, as the world falls apart for the likes of Eric and Felicia, the pastor is notified with the faint hope that there may be words....

The pastor meets the grieving family somewhere between the first cough and the last gasp. The dying can be arrow swift or painfully slow, but slow or fast we all return to dust. They say that fire and rust is, in a way, the same chemical reaction—oxidation. One is fast and one is slow, but the results are ultimately the same: The world falls apart.

For those who have gone through the torturous illness of a parent that Felicia has experienced, there is an image in the poem The Long Approach *by Maxine Kumin that may be helpful. She describes a chance conversation she had with a man sitting next to her on an airplane. He handled horses and was experienced in grooming and transporting thoroughbreds from racetrack to racetrack by plane. The elegant, stately animals, he explained, were loaded into a plane facing backwards so they could brace themselves during takeoffs, because any slip could damage those spindly, powerful (and valuable) legs. The landing was something else. Nothing could be done for the horses but to pray for calm weather and to "ask the pilot to make a long approach."*

WK

No More Hugs

Our physical and emotional bonds with our parents predate even our first breath on this earth. Before we squint up into those two, huge faces, we share our mother's food and blood. We kick her around a little. We already know her voice. Daddy's, too, if he talks to her tummy while we're in there. The DNA dance deals us our father's nose, our mother's hair. Whatever hopes and anxieties are ruling their world influence ours even before we make the one-way trip out of warm, wet darkness into the light. And modern psychology tells us that by the time we're five years old our personalities have already absorbed the imprint of our parents' dreams, fears and preferences. We live for their smiles and hugs. We want them to be proud of us. We struggle for their love.

Then, one day or night, death carries them off on another one-way trip out of sight, beyond our reach. Often, for the first time we are forced to face just what it has meant to be born the son or daughter of this man or that woman. Paradoxically, the loss of a parent finally forces us to acknowledge all that the relationship has and has not been. For some people, death provides the very first glimpse of their parent as a person separate from them, whose life had a beginning and an end, a destiny and a shape outside anyone's control.

Suddenly, absence reveals more clearly what was.

LOSING YOUR VERY BEST FRIEND
Tracey's Story

"Starbucks on Main. Can I help you?"

"Sorry, I must've dialed the wrong number."

Tracey dropped the receiver back into its cradle and fought hard to swallow the hot lump in her throat.

"Hey, Mom, you okay?" her daughter asked.

"I'm fine," Tracey said, and felt her jacket pocket for the keys. "All packed?"

"Yep. I decided to leave Goldie, though."

"You did? They'd let you keep a fish in the dorm, I'm sure."

"Yeah, but I don't think she'd survive the drive. We can't leave her in the car, the heat'd probably boil her, and I don't wanna be carryin' a fish bowl into every Burger King between Chicago and New Jersey."

"Okay, so *I'll* carry her inside," said Tracey. "You're gonna miss that fish, honey. It's the first one you didn't kill within the first two weeks."

"Well, that's the other thing, what with all the heavy dating I'm going to be doing at school…"

"Excuse me?"

"Mom, I'm kidding. Lighten up. What with all my classes and all the studying, I figure you'll do a better job keeping Goldie alive than I would. And I just don't need the death of another fish on my conscience."

"Who's going to feed her while I'm driving to Jersey and back?"

"I called Mrs. Curtis and asked her if she would do it when she picks up the mail."

"When did you do that? I was on the phone."

"I know, I used *my* phone."

"Oh."

"Hey, now *there's* something I could really use at college. How 'bout it, Mom?"

"The phone'll still be here when you come home for Thanksgiving."

"I thought you were going to think about letting me stay at school."

"I did and you aren't. Did you get the bag with those extra sheets we bought yesterday, and the…?"

"Comforter, the towels, the bathrobe, the extra blanket, the multiple vitamins, yes, yes, yes, Mom. We are fully loaded, ready to rock 'n' roll!"

"Good. Well then, let's blow this pop stand. Princeton awaits!"

Her daughter rolled her eyes, but she grinned with pride, too. They both let out a yelp of elated disbelief.

"My little girl in college," Tracey sighed for the both of them.

"Don't start crying again, okay?"

"I'm not," Tracey promised, "but you have to admit it's pretty awesome, isn't it?"

"Totally."

"God, I wish Gran could see you now."

"She can, Mom."

That hot lump in Tracey's throat had cooled a bit with all the talk of goldfish and telephones. But mentioning her deceased mother—even though she used her daughter's nickname for the old lady rather than calling her "Mother"—made Tracey choke on another geyser of tears that was even tougher to swallow. So she nodded quickly and herded her college-bound daughter out the door and into the SUV, rushing them away from the home her daughter was leaving for the first time, pulling out of the driveway so fast the front of the car scraped a little on the street.

The funny thing was, the two of them were driving instead of flying because Tracey wanted to stretch out the time she had left to spend with the last child to leave home. And yet she found herself darting ahead of other cars on the freeway, driving a little faster than usual, in an almighty hurry to put distance between herself and the "wrong number" that had shaken her to the core.

Her foot got heavier and heavier on the accelerator as she replayed and replayed again that cheerful greeting on the phone: "Starbucks on Main. Can I help you?"

Tracey had dialed a second time, more carefully than the first. "Starbucks on Main. Can I help you?"

"Sorry, I must've dialed the wrong number," is what Tracey had said, but the number she had dialed wasn't wrong. It was just no longer right. She had grown accustomed to dialing her mother's old number and listening to it ring on and on unanswered. She had come to derive an odd sort of comfort from the electronic purr repeating itself over and over.

A whole year after her mother's death, and still this silly little thought train trundled round in circles inside Tracey's head: *Just one more ring and she'll pick up...Just one more ring, and I'll hang up...Just one more ring....*

It was a hopeless and stupid exercise. Tracey knew that. She'd resist making the call for weeks at a time, and then something would happen or some memory would surface and the cycle of dialing and listening would resume.

She wasn't ready for her mother's phone number to be recycled, handed over to Starbucks or anybody else. No. Her mother's phone number should have been retired, like they retired Michael Jordan's 23. It wasn't fair. No one else should be able to dial those precious seven digits and find what they were looking for, not if Tracey couldn't.

The instant that strange Starbucks-voice came back at her over the phone line, an angry finger poked into the tenderloin of grief in Tracey's gut, and now she couldn't shove the ache from its stomping ground right below her rib cage. It had squatted down on top of all her empty-nester angst and had evidently dug in for a long roost.

There would be no more phone calls.

* * * * * * *

Plowing down the freeway, Tracey realized that she dialed her mother's number on days when she was happiest, on days when she was saddest, and on days—like today—when she was both.

"Slow down a little, Mom," her daughter said, putting a calm hand over Tracey's tense clench on the steering wheel.

Tracey checked the speedometer. "Good Lord." She took her foot off the accelerator. "Oh, boy."

"Why don't you let me drive the first leg?" her daughter suggested.

"Good idea."

Tracey pulled over. They each got out.

Halfway round the car they hugged each other and held on for a long time.

THE LAST VIEW
Kevin's Story

Kevin had always been pretty squeamish when it came to coffins, hearses and the like. He customarily gave them a wide berth. Graveyards gave him the willies when he drove past them, particularly at night. Though he was fascinated by their cool gray statuary and somewhat attracted by the gentle waves of green grass upon which all those imposing monuments swam—he preferred to leave anything that wrapped itself around death alone. He used to think that this discomfort was a hangover from too many late nights spent watching horror movies as a young kid. Those scary films had convinced him that spirits hung out in cemeteries and funeral homes, swimming around with a vague sense of discontent if not outright rage that they could no longer enjoy the luxuries of life as they had when they were living.

Kevin was just a little afraid that the dead were not quite dead.

So he steered clear of all the places and things that attempted to bind the dearly departed to the murky confines of death. He did not want to be haunted by anyone, and he figured that if he left the dead, their hangouts, and all their accoutrements alone, maybe they would leave him alone. Mortuaries, cemeteries, hearses, coffins, and—as an adult—even horror movies were all therefore off limits.

Though he had thought such things would hold death at bay, his father's passing proved that Kevin might run from its trappings but could never hide from its reality. In hindsight, it was easy to see that mortality had taken its time sneaking up on him.

When he was eight years old, Kevin had seen his father cut his thumb opening a can of tuna, and all that maroon life-juice spurting out of his dad made that impressionable little boy's mouth fall open.

When he was about eleven, he had seen his father stumble backwards over a curb, trying to avoid the boiling gusher of radiator fluid shooting up out of their overheated Buick. His dad fell quickly and landed hard. Kevin was hip to grown-ups' fragility by then, but it scared him to see his father out of control and vulnerable.

By the time disease had shrunk his father down to child-size, Kevin—now a young man—had wised up. His father's status as a mere mortal, subject to the law of gravity and a victim of cause and effect was clear: Smoke for decades, the Surgeon General promised, and you court a smoker's death. Pure and simple. As plain as the warning on the side of every pack of cigarettes.

But no law of physics or principle of causality, no surgeon's warning explained away the rage the young man felt watching his father shrink before his eyes. No mature perspective on the inevitability of death softened the edges of the horror Kevin faced one bright Sunday afternoon in the funeral parlor.

He didn't say anything, but he gave a little howl when he saw his father laid out, because he knew it wasn't his father anymore. He knew his father was gone and not coming back. That unforgettable sight introduced an entirely new principle for Kevin to digest. Death became as real and inexorable as the simplest mathematical equation: Father's body minus father's spirit equals that thing in the box.

That's death.

If he wanted, Kevin could reach out…and touch it.

Others did.

But Kevin didn't want to.

He sat on the other side of the room and stole glances at the body every once in a while. When others encouraged him to move closer to pray for his father's soul with the rest of the family, Kevin resisted coming any closer than several yards away.

He would pray right where he was.

After all, he was praying for Dad, right? Not for that thing in the box.

EACH OF US MOURNS
A DIFFERENT PARENT
Marie's Story

On her way up to the pulpit to give the eulogy, Marie gently stroked her father's casket. She may even have paused there for a moment, trying to absorb an extra dose of strength from him for the last public duty she would perform in his honor. She was the only one of four siblings who would speak, because his widow rightfully thought the rather large throng in attendance would want to hear from his best friend and a business associate as well. So Marie would distill his children's collective sense of loss down to three or four minutes of shared memories, and then she would take her seat.

Looking out from the pulpit at the people who had come from all over the city and the country to send her father off—most of them strangers to her—Marie knew that what she was about to say was true beyond all argument or qualification.

"Each of us is here mourning a different man," she began in a voice that grew stronger by the sentence. "It is in the nature of human beings to show a slightly different face to different people in different circumstances. There's a public face and a private face. Some of you knew my father as boss or as a business partner. Maybe you are a lifelong friend. Perhaps you knew him through public acclaim or through whispered rumor. Maybe he joked with you, maybe he cried with you. Most of you would call yourselves his friends. But perhaps a few of you were his foes…secretly, of course. And yet, here we all are together, paying our respects to a man we think we knew.

"But did any of us really know him? Do we really know the person who died?

"Even within a family—each individual child has a unique perspective on each parent, and that perspective shifts from day to day, age to age, through the giving and the taking, through the rebellions and the blissful coming-together times. So—even among us who knew him all our lives—the hole our father's departure has left in our hearts has a different shape, size and depth.

"I'll spend the next few minutes trying to broaden and deepen your understanding of who he was to me by sharing pieces of the father I knew. But I already know that will only comprise a pale shadow of the true man. I'll miss the mark by miles and miles, but I'll come as close as a loving daughter can.... "

Marie spent a little while alluding to events and describing qualities that many might have recognized. Then she shared remembrances that made the smaller circle of his family and friends nod and smile. She moved beyond those tales into revelations of moments she and her father had shared, favors and consolations they exchanged that no one knew anything about: the expensive circle skirt he bought for her when she was five years old, the patient way he taught her the cha-cha, the night he helped Marie nurse a finicky newborn.

When she had shared what she thought they needed to know, Marie stepped or staggered down from the pulpit, suddenly unsure in which direction her seat might be found. Someone lent her an arm upon which she could lean. She pressed her face into the padded shoulder of her husband's suit jacket. After the service, the pastor of the church, who had known her father well, confessed that he had learned more about who her father had been from what she had shared in those few minutes than the good priest had gleaned from face-to-face interaction with her father during all the years the two men had hung out together, playing chess and trading truisms—this from the man who had heard her father's confessions for decades!

But Marie wondered to herself if any of them truly knew the man they were about to bury. She remembered a night when the pain was particularly bad, when her father made a grimaced vow to use the medication's limitations as an opportunity to "Work out my salvation!" She had wondered what he meant by that, but she thought it too personal a question to ask. That was between her father and his God.

Right before the funeral, as she worked on multiple drafts of her eulogy, Marie had realized that only God really knew who had just died. Indeed, her father's death showed her how deep a mystery each human being is.

Marie now understood that no matter how close the ties or tight the family weave only God knows every crevice and peak of private territory within each inner man or woman. It was true for her father, true for Marie, true for every human alive.

For each person—one by one—comes out of God and eventually returns.

Each and every one of us, Marie understood now, are God's and God's alone.

Meditation

Tracey, Kevin and Marie are displaced persons who are finding that coping with the death of a parent is a full-time job without benefits. It is the memories that startle and surprise us when they rise to the surface. These memories may be triggered by an unanswered phone, a lifelong fear that never was attended, or a story we almost forgot. They catch us when we are keeping a stiff upper lip or maybe just sipping scotch.

A Catholic priest may quote a different Scripture than a Jewish rabbi. He may give a different interpretation than would a Protestant minister. So the "obsequies" (the final rituals for the dead) will have a denominational flavor depending on our cultural traditions. But the memories of our parents—these are non-denominational. They swell up to flood our eyes like a sudden squall.

Marie is right as rain when she says each person—one by one—comes out of God and eventually returns. Isn't that how memories work too? They come from God and, if we can follow them back as they fade into the sunlight, they seem to return to the Lord of memory for safe keeping.

WK

All This Stuff!

While we lived under their roof, there were closets we were not to enter. There were drawers we were not to open. There were safe deposit boxes, bank accounts, file cabinets, pantries, desks, storage spaces, workshops, offices, basements and attics that were off limits. Some we didn't even know existed.

Then one day, the "Do Not Enter" edicts are suddenly rescinded. What were once private affairs become public—at least to us as their offspring. What may have been hoarded for years suddenly becomes available. And usually some or all of what was theirs becomes ours.

The popular saying declares it aright: "You can't take it with you."

Our parents do not take their possessions with them. Nor can they carry away or destroy all the physical evidence of how they spent their time, how they indulged their delights, or how they sought to hide their flaws.

The spirit of our dear departed may leave terra firma, but what remains in the wake of that exit can reveal almost too much about who they were. Depending on how well they organized their lives, how well they made their "final arrangements," and how much control they sought to exercise over the "dividing of the spoils," sifting through a parent's belongings exposes a great deal about who that person was. It can also teach us a tremendous amount about who we have become.

Whether we like it...or not.

THEY CAN'T TAKE IT WITH THEM
Ben's Story

The door got stuck halfway open, but Ben had seen his father give it that extra little push with his shoulder often enough to know the remedy. He lifted the handle just enough to pull the bottom of the door up off the cement, pressed his weight against the cracked plank of warped plywood, and *presto*!

Un-chaperoned access to the old man's inner sanctum.

Suddenly Ben was trampling on lonely but hallowed ground. Dust particles blew in after him and twirled around in the sunlight like minuscule galaxies adrift in space. Sunlight had to fight to get the better of three months' of dank darkness. Ben waited for his eyes to adjust.

"What are you going to do with all of it?" his mother had just asked him over their turkey sandwiches and tomato soup.

"That depends on what's out there, Ma."

"He wanted Frank to have the tools."

"Frank can have the tools."

"Mary Ann's bicycle's still out there. He meant to fix it for her, you know, he just couldn't find the right…"

"Mary Ann has a new bike. We gave her one for Christmas last year."

"He wanted to fix the old one for her."

"I know, but she outgrew it pretty quick."

"His eyes. He just couldn't…"

"Someone at Salvation Army can fix it up for a kid who really needs it."

"You're right, you're right," she said, and got up from the kitchen table, wrapping up half her sandwich to eat later. "That's why you need to be doing this instead of me. I'd just hang on to everything, and it's time to let go."

36

"Time to let go," Ben repeated, looking around his father's dusty workshop. So he decided to get busy tossing out the junk.

Don't think, he told himself, just ditch: the broken rocker, the chain-less bike, the three-legged card table, the cans half-filled with dried up paint, the brushes that were stiff and worthless.

"Why even have a workshop, Pop, if you're not really going to…?"

Ben stopped himself from talking out loud to a dead man.

He opened the sticky door wider to let more light and fresh air in. He opened the four windows on the south wall, too, even though they complained bitterly that their previous steward saw no need to strain hinges, disturb spider webs, and stretch the thick ivy lacing time had taken years to weave over the window panes. Ben ignored their protests. The place needed air and light badly. Nobody could work in a tomb masquerading as a shed. No one.

He went around to the back of the house and dragged three large plastic garbage cans to the front of the shed. When he went back for the fourth, he discovered his mother watching from the kitchen window, looking older than he'd ever seen her. He sent her his best smile.

She waved and went back to washing up their lunch dishes.

Time to let go.

"Frank's not gonna want these," Ben grumbled, raking through his father's tool box. The tools were old and worn and dull. There wasn't an electric anything in the whole place, because his dad was not serious about working with his hands or building anything. When something around the house broke, his mother would have to pay somebody to come out and fix it. Ben could have done it for them, but his dad had this handyman image to protect. Ben had to chuckle just thinking about it. The old man was no workman. Before he retired, he had sold insurance to farmers up and down Route 57.

Ben was the real carpenter in the family.

Which is why the only well kept tools in his father's shed were the miniature hammer and the tiny little screwdriver Ben found in a small metal case labeled "Ben's Tool Set." It was tucked under the scuffed-up desk his father had placed under one of the windows he never opened. At first, Ben thought it was some kind of lunchbox, because it was small and a badly scarred but honest red. There was also a pretty ineffectual saw inside, with a flimsy blade that a nine year old boy might have found pretty thrilling. A few nails and screws rattled around in the bottom of the box.

Ben hadn't seen it in twenty years.

A piece of paper was scotch-taped inside the lid. He peeled it off carefully because it was yellow and brittle with age. Its folds were splotched with oil and something that looked like dark red paint, but the graphics and instructions were obviously the blueprint for a dog house—the very same dog house that was sitting outside the shop window, halfway between the house and the shed.

The little shelter had surrendered all its paint and a few of its shingles to time and weather, and its occupant was long, long gone—dead some fifteen years. But the worn out structure still played host to a childhood full of warm memories.

And one of them swept over Ben, catching him by surprise with its tender power. On a day not unlike this one, he had built a dog-house with an insurance salesman who split the thumbnail of his left hand wide open while pretending to be something he wasn't in order to impress a little boy who believed his Pop could do everything.

A KEEPSAKE OR JUNK?
Bob and Andrea's Story

"She wanted me to have the watch, Andrea."

"You?"

"Yes, me."

"And I suppose she told you she wanted you to have it."

"As a matter of fact, she did."

"When?"

"Thanksgiving last year, when she had us all over for dinner, she said…"

"She didn't have us *all* over, Bob."

"You never came, so she stopped inviting you."

"Actually, I remember it the other way around. She stopped inviting me, so I stopped coming."

"You drank too much, Andrea. You got loud."

"Right, messed up her Norman Rockwell photo-op."

"Yes, you did."

"So last Christmas, she tells you…"

"Last Thanksgiving."

"Whatever. She told you she wanted you to have her watch when she died?"

"Yep. Maybe she was prescient or something."

"Prescient?"

"Clairvoyant. You know. Maybe she saw it coming, maybe something inside her knew she was…"

"I *gave* her this watch, Bob! For her fiftieth birthday."

"Yeah? Well, maybe she forgot."

"I don't believe this."

"Well, you better, 'cause I'm taking it."

"Come on, it's a woman's watch. You're not going to wear it."

"She wanted me to give it to Diane."

"Why would she want your ex-wife to have her watch?"

"She wasn't my ex-wife at the time."

"Well, everybody knew she was going to be your ex. Even Mom with her classic case of denial-itis had to see that divorce coming. The two of you didn't stop fighting the whole time you were over here."

"How do you know? You weren't here."

"Roger told me."

"Little bugger's still a tattle-tale. Doesn't matter. She wanted Diane to have the watch. She said so."

"Why would she want that witch to have her watch?"

"They got along."

"I'll just bet they did. Birds of a feather..."

"I can't believe you said that."

"Yes, you can."

"You gonna dance on her grave tomorrow?"

"Haven't decided yet."

"Unbelievable."

"Well, if Diane's getting the watch I'm taking all the books, all the dishes and all the linen."

"Since when is one watch equal to all the, the..."

"Books, dishes and linen."

"Right, since when is one little watch worth all that?"

"The minute you give that stinkin' watch to your ex-wife, that's since when."

"You are something else, Andrea."

"*I'm* something else? You've already got the house to do with as you please."

"That's what she wanted."

"Of course, it is. You're her little prince, aren't you? You're the little man of the house, her pride and joy, her sweet little one and only."

"Why on earth didn't she leave a will?"

"She didn't think she'd ever die! People that mean never think they can die. They think they'll live forever, but they're wrong. The Grim Reaper's the only hope some of us victims have."

"You're breakin' my heart."

"Am I?"

"No."

"That's because you don't have one, because you're just like her."

"What're you doing with that?"

"This? It's a dish towel, Bob. You want the dish towel now?"

"Mom used to wipe her hands on that."

"Aw, please."

"And she'd use them instead of potholders, remember? She used to burn herself grabbing a dishtowel instead of a potholder to take the hot stuff out of the oven. Burned up a whole mess of towels over the years, too."

"That explains all the greasy, yucky brown crusties on it. Blech!"

"Don't throw that away!"

"You want it? You can dig for it."

"I don't get you. I know you and Mom didn't always get along, but…"

"That has got to be the understatement of the century."

"But she's dead, Andrea, she's not coming back. She's not going to be around anymore to pick on you or argue with you or make you cry. She's dead. And you're acting like she just grounded you for a week."

"Try a month."

"She never grounded you for a whole month."

"No? Well, I suppose she didn't give me this either."

"Oooh. Yikes."

"Maybe you remember this?"

"Oh, wow. You can still see where she…"

"And this?"

"Andrea…"

"I'm thirty-two years old, and I'm still wearing bangs to cover up that one."

"She had a temper."

"Is that what you call it?"

"She was different with you. I don't know why."

"I know why. She couldn't deal with competition. She didn't

want another woman around the house showing her up, looking better than her, cooking better than her, being better than her. You and Roger got off easy. Dad just sat in his chair and let her…"

"You know what they say, 'Women love their sons and raise their daughters.' She was just trying to keep you out of trouble."

"Oh, yeah. And what a great job she did, huh? My life's just one big trouble-free zone, isn't it?"

"Don't go, Andrea. We've got to finish going through all this stuff."

"You finish. I need a drink."

"C'mon. Don't go. You can have the watch."

"I don't want it. I don't want any of this junk."

"Andrea!"

"I'm going back to the hotel."

"Mother of God. My kingdom for a will!"

Meditation

"To the victor belong the spoils" is the last rule of war. "You can't take it with you" is the last rule of life. "The stuff belongs to the kids, and the stuff sometimes spoils." That is the sad experience Ben, Bob and Andrea are going through.

There is nothing more distasteful than when siblings argue over what belongs to whom. A Wisconsin farmer told me that he felt the most important thing he had done for his family was to call in a lawyer to go over the legalities of the transmission of the family farm. All the family was present. Contracts were read, understood, agreed to and signed. It seems the rule of law is necessary even in the family.

The often comic reading of the will can make public for laughs all the greed and viciousness that usually stays unseen within a family. This is often followed by an explosion as the spoils are divided one by one. I think of minefields and radioactive debris.

It is the stuff that dreams (and nightmares) are made of.

WK

The Family Tree Loses a Branch

A hurricane blows the roof off your house, and suddenly overhead there is nothing but white clouds and blue sky—or an ominous dome of darkness. Everything inside is now outside, exposed, vulnerable. And all that you hoped to keep at bay on the other side of sturdy walls, well, all of that comes crashing in on rooms desperate for shelter against the elements.

It can feel like that when a mother or father passes away.

My, oh, my, but it definitely feels like that when they're *both* gone!

When a parent dies, the family tree sheds a branch or a limb. And yet, paradoxically, all the twigs and leaves remain, as it were, suspended in midair.

What happens to them? To what do they cling? How do they maintain their connection to their tree, their roots, the earth and all the wet nourishment upon which they depend?

The metaphors just keep coming.

I've often described a family as the garden God decides to plant each of us in, so that we might best fulfill the mysterious divine plan. When a parent dies, it seems as if the Master Gardener has come through our midst, on a stroll or a march, and has pulled up the oldest, tallest stalk among us—the one whose seeds made our very lives possible. And having pulled that old plant up by the root, the divine gardener walks off to transplant it in fields beyond our knowing.

Does any one among us who remain have leaves broad enough to replace the shade we've just lost?

LOSING A GENERATION
Ronnie's Story

"Testing, one, two, three, four. I'm sorry, is this on?"

Dreadlocks, cornrows and weaves bobbed up and down throughout the ballroom, but a table full of crisply pressed, silver-haired folk sitting in the back row of banquet tables shook their heads from side to side.

Who seated all the old folks so far back, Ronnie wanted to ask, but didn't. He gave a nod to his cousin Bo—the sound technician, deejay and master vibe jockey for the evening. The microphone gave an unbearable squeal that might easily have set dogs three counties away to howling. It finally mellowed into a robust hum.

"Is that better?" Ronnie boomed at the silver heads specifically.

Several denture-heavy smiles grinned back at him. Someone gave a wave.

"Good," Ronnie said as he cleared his throat and unfolded the paper napkin full of notes he'd jotted down at the picnic. "What a weekend, huh? What a game this afternoon. That was the first time the ladies beat the men, wasn't it?" He was stalling for more time while he pulled out his reading glasses. "Softball ain't as soft as it used to be, huh, fellas?"

Cousin Edna stood up and led the ladies in a loud series of "Whoop, whoop, whoops," pumping her well-defined biceps for all to see. That golden strike-out arm looked slightly incongruous sprouting from the sleeveless, chiffon evening dress she'd obviously paid a pretty penny to buy.

The lady softball players' self-congratulatory applause died out faster than Ronnie thought it would and left a gulf where his opening comments were supposed to be. He squinted hard at the words scrawled on his picnic napkin. He could barely make out the words "Welcome, everybody!"

Just as he opened his mouth to say that, Cousin Grace got up from the table right in front of his podium, her dinner plate in hand. Ronnie's newly enhanced microphone sent her ravenous sigh into the ballroom's farthest corner.

"Don't know who Betty Jo got to cater this shindig," she told her table partners, "but whoever done it, them puppies really nailed the sweet potato pie this year. Hallelujah, praises to ya."

And with that, she carried her plate over to the buffet line for another slice. The pilgrimage itself was distracting enough, but her culinary review got a bigger hand than Ronnie had when he stepped up to the podium. In self defense, he folded it into his remarks.

"Grace is right, folks, let's give the cooks a round of applause, shall we?"

They did, but now it was official: Ronnie was stalling.

Why had they picked him out of all the cousins to be master of ceremonies? He was an accountant for God's sake, in love with his little ten feet by ten feet cubicle and computer screen full of numbers. Just sitting in the midst of a crowd made him feel as if he were choking. He dreaded having to speak in public under any circumstances, and the reunion's sprawl of family was nothing but an audience with a carte blanche license to criticize.

His dad had been the ham—the frustrated entertainer, the emcee from birth. Ronnie wasn't that man. That suave charmer was no more. Why had Ronnie ever agreed to try to fill those shoes? It was hopeless.

"We have a lot of people to thank for making this reunion our best ever," he said, struggling to get back up on top of his master-of-ceremonies duty. "I'm sure to forget some people if I try listing them all. So I'm leaving that honor for Betty Jo Williams. She can definitely tell you what everybody did."

"And just how long it took 'em to do it, too," Betty Jo chimed in.

"I know that's right," somebody said.

"I'm sure," said Ronnie, eager to get this done and over with. "I'm here to welcome everybody and to thank so many of you for coming so far to be part of the first Ellis Family Reunion of the Third Millennium!"

"Everybody ain't here!" his aunt piped up from that back table full of old folks, loud enough for the whole ballroom to hear. Somebody tried to shush her, but Sister Rose just spoke up louder. "Everybody didn't make it to no third whatchamacallit!"

"That's right," Cousin Grace said, around the delicious mush of sweet potato in her mouth. "Sister Rose sure 'nough right about that."

"Yes, Auntie's right, of course," Ronnie said, clearing his throat a second time. "Some of us," he couldn't mention his father by name or the jig would be up, for sure, "some of us have gone home to glory, and we're going to pay our respects to…"

"What's he know 'bout 'goin' home to glory?'" Sister Rose yelled from the back table. "My brother's dead!" she cried. "My baby brother!"

One of the other silver heads fought his way to his feet and tried to lift the old lady up with him. No luck. She wasn't finished calling it like it was.

"That boy's daddy! Dead as a door nail!" she said, beating at the hands that tried to corral her. "Dead as this here table!"

"My Lord, my Lord!" someone said, and heads started shaking and nodding all over the room. A few people raised their hands to heaven.

"My baby brother ain't here for no third whatever, he ain't here at all, is he?"

A head full of braids swung their way over to the silver-heads' table, and Cousin Edna carried her pumped-up biceps over there as well, both relatives ready to give Sister Rose a full escort to the ladies room.

"Go on, Ronnie," Betty Jo Williams prompted from her seat up on the dais where all the reunion organizers were seated. "She'll be all right."

"Y'all leave me be, ya hear?" Sister Rose said, shooing the young ones off. She dabbed at her eyes with a beautiful white handkerchief and got to her feet on her own steam, leaning on her cane and the arm of the silver-haired gentleman who was first to lend his arm.

"Just go on back to your seat," she said to the young ones. "Eat your bellies full to poppin' like you don't know what I'm talkin' 'bout. You'll find out soon enough. Time'll teach ya."

Betty Jo wanted the disturbance to quit spoiling the party, so she urged the emcee on one more time, with a lot less patience in her tone. "I said go on, Ronnie."

But Sister Rose wasn't quite done making her point. "That ain't Ronnie! Everybody in here know that's Ronnie, *Junior*, up there," she said on her cane-assisted way out of the ballroom. "That ain't the real Ronnie." She stopped and faced the room for emphasis. "The real Ronnie's dead! All my beautiful brothers! Every last one of 'em. Lord, have mercy, how come You took 'em all?"

"Come on, Rose," whispered the silver gentleman at her arm.

"I'm the oldest, I should've gone first," said Rose, but she was on the move again, like a slow train heavy with sorrow. The ballroom door shut behind her, but the whole banquet crowd heard her cry, "Lord took 'em all and left me here! How come? How come He done that?"

Sniffles filled the silence. Lots of dinner napkins did handkerchief duty.

"Ronnie, you go on, boy," Betty Jo said to the forty-year-old tax accountant at the microphone, softer this time. She was standing right behind him with a gentle hand on his back. "You go on. Do your daddy proud."

"You can do it," Cousin Bo said from behind his sound station.

But it was no use. Ronnie shook his head, folded up his napkin full of notes and barbecue stains, and picked his way between tables on a path to follow his aunt.

"Well!" someone moaned as he passed.

Another relative reached out to squeeze his hand. "That's all right, baby."

"God's ways be higher than our ways!"

"Past all understandin'!"

Ronnie closed the ballroom door behind him and leaned back

against it, trying to rein in his feelings. He listened as this evening's banquet ceremony became tomorrow morning's church service, with Betty Jo praying and the banquet hall sprouting calls for mercy. Evidently, Cousin Grace had put down her fork and taken up the microphone, for he heard her sweet contralto swing down low to start a hymn.

"Pardon me, sir," a waiter said, and politely stepped around him.

A parade of service folk then slipped by the accountant on their way in with the dessert trays and coffee. Ronnie took a deep breath and moved on down the hotel corridor on a hunt for his aunt. He needed a dose of her reality. He needed someone to recognize the epidemic of disappearances that was decimating his family. He needed to be with someone who felt just as abandoned and helpless as he did.

But where was she? Where had that silver haired man taken her?

Ronnie went to the ladies room and knocked on the door, calling her name. No one answered. He tried to remember what hotel room his aunt was in, but figured she probably hadn't taken a room since she lived just outside of town. Maybe she was headed home. He rode down in the elevator, avoiding the eyes of curious guests, counting the floors one by one, afraid he'd be too late.

He found Rose sitting in one of the wingback chairs across from the bell captain's desk, calm and safe under the watchful eye of that man who looked so much like someone Ronnie used to know or wanted to know…or both.

Rose's escort seemed glad to see him, too. "Ain't a whole lot of her crowd left, is there?" the gentleman said, as the two men shook hands.

"No," said Ronnie, "not many."

Up close like this, Ronnie could see that the man was thirty years younger than his aunt, which placed him somewhere around a well-preserved sixty. Ronnie was embarrassed that he didn't know who this relative was, and he felt too ashamed to ask. Was he a distant uncle, a second or third cousin? Was he family by marriage?

"I'm just a friend," the silver head said, sensing Ronnie's confusion. "Just a friend from church, that's all," and he gave a name

Ronnie immediately forgot. What he would never forget, however, was the sad smile on that man's face as he looked at the old woman sitting with her hands folded in her lap, her gaze lost in vistas neither of them could see. "Me and Mother Rose warm the same pew on Sundays, don't we?" he said to her, not really expecting an answer.

He didn't get one either.

Ronnie watched the gentleman's eyes grow moist.

"How's the sayin' go?" said Rose's friend. "Old age ain't for sissies." He chuckled a little and gave Ronnie a wink. "If you'll sit here with her, I'll go 'round and get the car."

"Yes, sir, I will," Ronnie said, reverting to that wonderfully respectful courtesy he'd been trained to show so many years ago. "I'll sit right here 'til you come back."

"Good."

"And if it's okay with you, sir, I wouldn't mind riding home with her. Maybe I could help tuck her in or something. I'm her nephew, you know."

"I know. She told me. Sometimes she remembers, and sometimes..."

"You won't have to drive me back either. I can catch a cab back to the hotel," Ronnie assured him. "Maybe I'll spend the night at Aunt Rose's house."

"Oh, I don't think they'd let you do that," the man said. "They ain't got a place for family to sleep over, I don't think."

"I thought you were taking her home."

"To *the* home, son. Rose ain't lived on her own for quite a while now."

Ronnie looked at his father's oldest sister, staring off into space. "Oh."

"But you could sit up with her for a while," said her friend. "That'd be fine."

Ronnie nodded.

"Be back in a flash," the old man said with a smile like a benediction.

Watching him head out the sliding doors for the parking lot,

Ronnie decided he was going to apologize before asking that man his name again. But he'd remember it the second time. Maybe he'd get his phone number and address, too. That gentleman and Ronnie, Senior would have been about the same age.

Ronnie sat down in the wingback chair beside his aunt, took one of her hands in his own, and kissed it.

She came back from her far away spot in the past, looked at the handsome young man holding her hand, and asked him if he'd known her baby brother, Ronnie Ellis. "Boy up and passed away on me a month ago," she said.

The tax accountant—who slid south of the Mason Dixon Line for funerals and reunions only—smiled at his aunt and gave her ninety-year-old hand a tender pat.

"Well, ma'am," he said, "I'm really sorry to hear your brother passed. Why don't you tell me something about him? Looking at you, I know he must've been one fine man."

WHO'S GOING TO BE GRANDMA NOW?
Helen's Story

"Need some help in there?"

Jack entered the kitchen just as the second pumpkin pie hit the trash.

"Helen! What the…?"

The third and last pumpkin pie bit the dust.

"Honey, what are you doing?" Jack half-cried, half-whispered, not wanting to alarm the dining room full of guests. "Oh, my God," he said, looking into the garbage compactor. "What did The Great Pumpkin ever do to you?"

He carefully lifted the third pumpkin pie off the top of the heap. The others were too mangled to be rescued. Thank God he had done as he was told and kept the compactor's basket emptied throughout dinner preparations. A fresh white Glad bag had saved the day. Thank God Helen hadn't begun the massacre by tossing…

"Oh, no," Jack said. "Not the pecan pie."

"I am destroying the evidence," Helen said, sliding the pecan pie toward the edge of the kitchen counter, the garbage compactor's maw yawning below.

"Wait…" Jack cried, lifting the pie beyond her reach. "Why in God's name are you in here trashing dessert?"

"That is not dessert, it's evidence," said Helen, "and I'm getting rid of it!"

She reached for the pie again. But Jack held it up over his head.

"Stop being tall, Jack."

"You stop being short."

"I am not short, I'm petite. Now give me that pie."

"I have been waiting all year for this pie, Helen. I tread-milled my way down five pounds to make room around my middle for this pie, and you are not going to deny me my most treasured

Christmas tradition."

"It's my pie, and I'll trash it if I want to."

"No, it's your *party* and you'll cry if you want to. Leave my pie alone."

Helen crossed her eyes at him. Her husband was master of the lame joke.

Jack sang a couple bars of Leslie Gore's oldie-but-goodie from their courting days, but clearly Helen didn't remember it as well as he. Her face held on to its sullen, stewing brew of ticked-off wife mask, so he tried to refresh her memory with a few more bars and a gleeful, "Leslie Gore, you know, 1965 or thereabouts."

"If you're trying to make me laugh, Jack, I promise it will not work."

And with that she shoved the retrieved pumpkin pie back into the compactor.

Jack moaned. Things were worse than he thought. "Okay," he said, settling down for serious negotiations. He started to plant his pecan treasure on top of the refrigerator where his "petite" wife couldn't retrieve it without a step ladder. But evidently fridge top space was a dumping ground for kitchen kitsch Helen didn't need but couldn't toss. The rest of the kitchen was wall-to-wall food preparation, not a square foot of empty space in sight—except the pie-killing zone. So, Jack elected to hang on to the pecan pie for dear life. "You want to explain to me why you're in here murdering pastries?"

"I told you. The pies are evidence."

"Evidence of what?"

"The texture's probably not right. The crust's probably not flaky enough. Maybe I used too many pecans, or maybe not enough."

"This pie is always bliss on a fork, what are you talking about?"

"I tried to do it a little different. I used somebody else's recipe this year."

"Why on earth would you want to do that?"

"Just give it to me, Jack."

"Not until you tell me what's going on. The pie is evidence of what?"

"I have committed a heinous crime," Helen said quietly.

"What crime?" Jack asked, with a smug, little smile blooming around the edges of his question. She was calmer. He thought patient reason was winning the day, so he was completely unprepared for the painful shriek of Helen's answer.

"I...am...not...my...MOTHER!"

"Shhhh, honey," said Jack, "they're going to hear you."

"Like I care," Helen said, tossing the dish towel at the sink.

A cloud of suds splashed up on the African Violets she'd been nursing into bloom, but she didn't even notice. That's when Jack knew the situation was critical.

Helen plunked herself down at the kitchen table, her face in her hands. "I told you this would happen," she said quieter than before. "I told you having them all here for Christmas would be a disaster."

Jack set his precious pecan pie down on the counter, yes, in the killing zone. It didn't matter anymore. His wife was crying.

"It's not a disaster," he told her.

"They hate everything!"

"They do not hate everything."

"So, what have they liked? Can you tell me that?"

"Everybody seemed to like their presents this year."

"Beyond the booty, Jack," Helen cried, her volume rising again. He put his fingers to his lips.

She lowered her voice again, "The turkey's too dry, the dressing doesn't have enough sage, I fixed rice instead of mashed potatoes..."

"Those are persnickety, little..."

"Our tree's too small, the house doesn't smell like sugar cookies, we don't have a fireplace, Mom always had a Nativity out on the front lawn and we've got Santa and the reindeer, we went to ten o'-clock instead of Midnight Mass, we opened presents on Christmas Eve instead of Christmas morning..."

"Just a few for the kids."

"Mom's house had beds for everybody, real beds. In case you hadn't noticed, ours doesn't. And Felicity doesn't like sleeping with Olivia, Izer doesn't like bunking with Patrick, Nancy can't believe we won't let her sleep in the same room with her common law what's-his-name…"

"Leo."

"Whatever."

"Your mother wouldn't let her do that either."

"Ah, but we're supposed to be hip, we're supposed to be with it. Forget the example she's setting for her nieces and nephews."

"I don't know why the two of them don't just go and get married, you know? They've been together for how long now?"

"Don't try to change the subject," Helen said, slipping her shoes off for half a second. "I'm on a roll."

"You certainly are," said Jack. He sat down at the table next to her and pulled one of her tired feet into his lap for a massage.

"Stop trying to make me feel better," Helen said, while lifting her other foot into his lap.

"Who's trying to make you feel better?" he grinned.

"Where was I?" she moaned: her husband really knew his way around toes.

Over her shoulder, Jack could see the kitchen's swinging door crack open. Leo's eyes asked permission to enter. Jack shook his head no and smiled as he helped his wife pick up where she'd left off, "You were saying that Nancy wants to sleep with common-law Leo, but you won't let her."

Leo's jaw dropped…and he eased the door shut again.

"They all knew how much room we had. We talked about it ad infinitum over long distance."

"I've got the phone bills to prove it," Jack whispered to her big toe.

"And everybody said this was the place."

"Well, it is the biggest," he said. "Made sense to come here."

"But it's *not* big, Jack."

"I didn't say it was big. I said it was the biggest. It's a real house, for goodness' sake," Jack said with no small amount of pride. "Everybody else lives in an apartment or some high-rise condo-thing—no yard, no basement, no family room."

"They knew what the sleeping arrangements were going to be

like," Helen said, surrendering to a whine. "They agreed to the whole thing. And now Curtis and Jeanette hate sleeping on the sofa bed in the den because the kids wake them up watching cartoons in the morning. Barbara and Jeff keep saying they should have stayed in a hotel, even though everybody knows they couldn't afford it."

"They're saying that, hon, because they can see how hard you're working trying to keep everybody happy."

"They're saying it because they're miserable, Jack."

"They knew it would be a tight fit, hon, and they still wanted to come."

"What they wanted was to have someone else do all the work."

Jack looked around at the kitchen full of dirty dishes he'd have to cram into the dishwasher, the pots he'd have to wash. He studied the tile floor dusty with flour and stray onion peels he'd have to sweep. Maybe dodging work *was* part of the reason others elected to come their way this year, but it would have been dangerous to hand Helen any more fuel by agreeing with her.

"And here's the *coup de grace*, the real joy-killer for Christmas this year…"

"Yes, yes," he said, starting the second foot's massage, "I'm all ears."

"It doesn't snow in Southern California."

"So?"

"Christmas in Minnesota is white. Christmas here is palm trees and smog."

"They hated the snow."

"I know."

"They hated the cold."

"I know."

"They wanted to go to Universal Studios. They wanted to go to the beach. They came here to thaw out, for God's sake."

"I know, but now they miss the snow. They miss the cold. They miss the slush and the mess and the colds they always took home with them from Mom's place. They miss all the stuff they used to hate."

The kitchen door opened a second time, and their seven-year-old daughter came in carrying her Barbie and wearing a long face. Helen braced herself for another complaint, but the little girl just crawled up on her mother's lap and rested her head on Helen's shoulder. In another year or so she'd be too big to do that.

Jack and Helen looked at each other. Jack shrugged.

"Mommy?" said their daughter, wrapping her arm around Helen's neck.

"What is it, sweetie?" Helen asked her daughter.

"I miss Nanna," the little girl said.

Helen gave a little gasp and wrapped her arms around her daughter.

Jack patted his little girl's back but looked straight at his wife. "There's a lot of that goin' around, honey. Pretty contagious stuff, I'd say."

He got to his feet, shoved the pecan pie into the compactor, and gave his wife a wink. "If it ain't your recipe, baby, I'm not eatin' it."

Helen watched her husband push through the kitchen door into the dining room. She loved the way he told Nancy, "You've got coffee duty. Leo, my man, you've got a hot date with a broom."

She gave her daughter one more hug. "Hey, sweetie, how 'bout some cookie dough ice cream?"

Meditation

Helen and Ronnie both lost giants. I suppose we think of our parents as giants because they were so big when we were so small. That's part of it. But the death of a parent can also provide a year's worth of stories for a TV sitcom, endless material for therapy sessions, subject matter for a full schedule of family reunions, and the constant intrusion into our consciousness of small reminders of who we are and where we came from.

Each of us has his or her own stories. Don't get me started. Okay, well, when my father's funeral Mass was over, his pastor invited us all down to the church basement before we drove out to the cemetery. Dad waited patiently in the hearse while the rest of us feasted on corned beef sandwiches—a surprise gift from the pastor in tribute to my father. Then the priest pulled another surprise and broke out the bourbon. I'm sure my father felt honored, even though he could not partake (being dead and all). My family and my father's friends immediately came to the conclusion that the corporal work of mercy of giving drink to the thirsty (us) was a higher priority than the corporal work of mercy of burying the dead (my dad). The result was that the funeral procession had to stop three times due to fender benders!

All these stories and all these dreams come from our heart. Sometimes people have guilt feelings about how they were not appreciative enough of their parents. Those guilt feelings do not come from the heart. Sometimes people have a tough time forgiving their parents after they are gone. That resentment doesn't come from the heart, either. But the stories and dreams do come from the heart, for Jesus said, "Where your treasure is, there also will your heart be" (Matthew 6:21).

WK

When It Wasn't All
Love and Kisses

You may not want to read this section, especially if you had a warm, uncomplicated bond with your parents. On the other hand, you may need to read it, either for yourself or to help you understand the conflicted emotions many others endure as they mourn. These next few stories acknowledge the special pain suffered by those whose relationships with their mother or father were fraught with tensions and wounds that may not have healed before death intervened.

Common sense and common experience tells us that into every parent-child relationship at least a *little* rain must fall. But "Medea" and "King Lear" aren't classics for nothing. Sometimes, instead of love, something else springs up between parent and child. Emotional and physical abuse, alcoholism and incest are real family killers, and they invade a great many homes. We should all pray every day for children who endure such agony. For them, childhood ends before it begins. The little person sprouts into a grown-up almost in self defense, trying to protect himself or herself (and maybe even some siblings) from the beast-in-parental-clothing.

Eventually, these children's bodies—like their souls—mature. They become adults, and one day their parents die. How ironic it must be to realize that even a parent who did not love you must still be buried and mourned. How unfair it must seem for others to expect you to be sad on a day that paradoxically sets you free. How difficult it must be to honor your true feelings when friends, clergy, even your own relatives may not.

Your family may have been spared major dysfunctional disasters, but even the widespread experience of parental divorce leaves a wound that can open again when a parent dies—complicating funeral arrangements, unearthing resentments and pain you may have thought had been laid to rest.

There is also the trial faced by adults who have lived under the shadow of one or both parents—never sure of any decision that lacked parental approval, never free to be who they are.

A parent's death can expose fractures within the family no one had to admit were there...until now.

THEY LIVED TOGETHER BUT DIED APART
Richard's Story

"We'll take good care of her, Mr. Ditillo."

"Thank you, I appreciate that," said Richard, running his hand through his thinning hair. "I'll come over later on this afternoon to pick out the…the…"

Try as he might, he couldn't say "casket."

"Oh, you don't have to do that today, sir," the funeral director told him.

"I know, but…"

"Why don't you go home? Get some rest. If you don't mind my saying so, that cold sounds pretty bad."

"It's a doozy, isn't it?" Richard said, pulling out his handkerchief to blow his nose. "My girlfriend's been shoving Echinacea down my throat for days. Echinacea pills, Echinacea tea, Echinacea juice."

"You don't want to get really sick right now," said the voice of experience. "Won't help things. Be good to yourself. This can wait a day or two."

"I think I'd rather, you know, keep moving," said Richard.

"I understand," the undertaker said. "Whatever's best for you."

Richard shoved his hands into his pockets, steeling himself for the duties that remained. Like a good watchman, he stood outside the nursing home's sliding glass doors and watched the mortuary van roll down the freshly paved driveway onto the tree-lined street. It passed a school bus picking up a group of little kids and then wheeled around a corner out of sight. Not quite ready to go back inside, Richard watched the school bus doors embrace the last student and lumber off in his mother's wake, until it too disappeared from view.

Richard took a deep breath and choked on the chill. A stiff

breeze reminded him that he'd stepped outside without a coat or jacket. The day promised to be crisp, to say the least. Two back-to-back sneezes reminded him he was fighting a doozy of a cold, so he walked back into the nursing home for the very last time, promising himself he would pack up his mother's things, pay the bill, and never see the inside of this place again. In fact, as the sliding glass doors whooshed shut behind him, Richard's mind got busy plotting a new route to work that would guarantee he'd never again have to pass by this tall brick building with its rolling green lawn and immature trees a decade away from providing decent shade.

"Sorry for your loss," the night janitor said on his way out the door at the end of his shift.

"Thanks, Jack," Richard said. "See you," came out of his mouth automatically, but the men shook hands knowing that would never happen.

The nurses manning the station on his mother's floor offered Richard coffee and a sweet roll. They knew how long he'd been there. Still, he turned down the refreshment. He should have been hungry but he wasn't. He should have been tired, but he was way past that. Somewhere deep inside, Richard suspected he would feel like this for days, weeks maybe: starving, but not hungry; exhausted, but not tired; full of so much feeling, yet empty at the core.

His mother's night nurse was pulling on her coat, ready to go home, but she stopped to give Richard a warm, strong hug.

She smelled of rubbing alcohol and body fluids with a small trace of flowery perfume sweetening the mix. For the brief instant that she held him, Richard was a little afraid he might throw up on her. She was such a rich mix of all the odors that had swamped him for days, making it hard to breathe, carving every moment into his sense memory, making the whole ordeal simultaneously vivid and deadening. Maybe the coffee and sweet roll would have stopped his stomach from churning.

Why did she hold on to him so long? When would she ever let him go? He was seconds away from baptizing her winter coat with last night's nursing home feast of macaroni and chocolate pudding when the woman released him and smiled.

All of a sudden, Richard found himself wishing she'd hug him again. Or at least he wished he had hugged her back. This nurse had a smile that could sweeten any sour stomach, quiet any inner storm. He'd seen her sedate a good many patients with that smile, including his mother. Now she was turning its "peace, be still" on him, and he was grateful.

"Thank you for last night," he said, and coughed back the warm flood that tried to fill his throat and eyes with tears.

This Florence Nightingale had made his mother's last hours less of a nightmare for Richard—telling him what would happen before it did, not leaving him alone when it was clear the end was close. She wore a small rhinestone cross Richard had considered pretty tacky, but last night she kept holding it with one hand and patting his mother's arm with the other, and he'd known she was praying his mother home. Good thing, too, because Richard sure as hell wasn't up to it.

"You take care of yourself," she said.

"You, too," said Richard, making a mental note to send her some flowers.

"Try some honey and lemon for that throat," she said and laughed a little. "You sound like George Burns."

"A shot of whiskey wouldn't hurt either," the nurse behind the desk offered.

"Nah, times like these, once you start in drinking," the night nurse warned, "you might not know when to stop." She gave him a knowing look, wrapped a bright blue scarf around big hair, and disappeared down the hall.

Richard was relieved to find his mother's roommate, Mrs. Jennings, sleeping soundly. His mother had slipped away quietly, but for some reason Mrs. Jennings awakened at that precise moment, just in time to be the first to get the news. The old lady had chattered away while Richard waited for the funeral home people. She babbled all sorts of religious stuff meant to be comforting, but Richard wondered who needed solace more—the bereaved son or the surviving dowager who seemed to be doing her own slow countdown. She was much healthier than Richard's mom, of course, and she had a husband and kids and grandkids visiting every five minutes.

All Richard's mother had was him and his latest girlfriend and memories that didn't seem all that comforting.

The room smelled mildly of disinfectant, and his mother's bed had already been changed. There was a medium-sized cardboard box resting on the bed, waiting for him to fill it with personal effects. He had packed it half full when the phone on his mother's bed-table rang. Richard picked it up quickly, fearing it would awaken Mrs. Jennings and start her sympathetic soliloquy all over again.

He could barely whisper into the phone at first. He coughed to clear his throat, but it didn't help much. "Hello," he said, still sounding like George Burns.

"May I speak with Mrs. Ditillo?"

There was a silence. A long one.

"Hello?" the man's voice said again, "Hello?"

"Yes," said George Burns, suddenly more than glad to stand in for Richard and take this call.

"Is this Marguerite Ditillo's room?" the man on the phone needed to know.

"Yes. Yes, it is," said George Burns.

"May I speak to her please? This is Fred Ditillo calling."

George Burns told Fred Ditillo that his ex-wife had passed away last night.

Yes, it was too bad he hadn't called earlier.

No, she did not suffer, but then cancer is never quick, is it?

Maybe Mr. Ditillo hadn't known she was ill. Oh, he did know? Her sister had told him. Still, it was hard to find the time to call. Yes, George Burns understood. An expensive plane ticket probably made a visit just too much of an investment. Sure.

Yes, it was a shame he'd missed her. She probably would have liked to speak to him, too. Before she died.

No, Mrs. Ditillo was not alone when she passed, George Burns told Fred. Her son Richard was with her to the end.

Oh, Richard was his son, too? Well, well.

Yes, the caller could probably reach his son at home, but he'd have to call back and ask the nurses at the floor station for the number.

Uh-huh, divorce is a terrible thing, and sometimes a second marriage needs to be protected from the first. Did George Burns know that?

Oh, sure, George Burns had a girlfriend who needed to be protected from his ex-wife. He knew firsthand how messy swapping one woman for another could get.

Fred Ditillo felt somehow compelled to explain to George Burns that he and his ex-wife had ended their messy marriage fifteen years ago. That was plenty time for both of them to go their separate ways. And even though Fred was the only one to remarry, he was certain his former wife had moved on into other attachments, other commitments.

But George Burns didn't think so.

If she'd moved on to other "attachments," why was her son the only one at her bedside when she drew her last breath? And even if she had attachments up the ying-yang, didn't Mr. Ditillo think that—having been married for twenty-some years—saying a proper goodbye was the least an ex-husband could do for a dying old lady who kept mumbling his miserable name?

"Excuse me?" the ex-husband said. "To whom am I speaking?"

Richard lowered the receiver back into its cradle. He lifted it again, called the nurse's station, and told them that they should not, under any circumstances, give out his home phone number to anyone.

"We wouldn't do that, Mr. Ditillo."

"Good," said Richard.

"We'd just take their number and let you know who called."

"Good."

Richard hung up again and finished packing up his mother's belongings. He paid the bill and marched out of the nursing home, with more than a cold's fever dampening his brow with sweat.

Slipping the cardboard box onto the backseat of his car, he vowed to leave the machine on at home and screen his calls for a while…just in case his father got another bout of the guilties and tried to track his son down.

MOURNING THE PARENT YOU HAD AND THE ONE YOU'LL NEVER HAVE
David's Story

The loud "kalumphf!" when he closed the front door told David's wife what she needed to know: He had not been given the promotion.

Molly immediately started fuming.

Her husband was much too sweet and even-tempered a guy to become outraged over the destructive stupidity of others, especially if he was the victim. If anybody was going to get ticked on his behalf, it would have to be Molly. So she immediately started calling his co-workers down at the warehouse self-serving idiots, backstabbing manipulators and various forms of expletive-deleteds.

The nerve of those guys! The greedy, power-grabbing nerve!

Molly checked her makeup again in the vanity's mirror. The sudden flush of anger precluded any need for additional blush, so she gave herself an extra spray of David's favorite perfume. They could still go out to dinner, she decided, pulling on a pair of heels for the first time since the funeral. A gravesite souvenir of caked-on mud smudged up the toe of her right shoe, but it rubbed off clean.

Molly could hear David moving through the foyer. She waited for his keys to crash-land on the dining room table and listened as his jacket found its hanger in the hall closet. Those familiar sound effects were punctuated by a second "kalumphf!" as her husband closed the closet door louder than usual.

They were going out, that's all there was to it. They had to go out.

Molly couldn't remember the last time they'd been anywhere other than the local family restaurant, their three children in tow. The two of them had eaten a lot of meals together in the hospital cafeteria during his mom's last two weeks, but that could hardly qualify as recreational dining. So that afternoon Molly had taken the kids over to her sister's house for the night. She'd soaked herself clean and sweet-smelling, and those so-and-sos at the factory were not going to deep-six their first night out in ages. It was bad enough they were trying to beat the self-confidence out of the company's very best worker. She wasn't going to let them get away with wrecking his marriage, too.

Forget about the promotion, she silently rehearsed her speech to him. *Forget about company loyalty and being rewarded for years of good service. None of that means anything anymore, David. Everybody knows that.*

Everybody except her husband, the world's last honest-to-God good guy.

He was headed for the kitchen…the fridge.

The beer can popped and sighed its painkiller promise into the air.

Molly decided then and there she was going to order champagne with dinner. That's what a man like David deserved to be drinking tonight. That's what he needed after all he'd been through. Molly had some petty cash stashed away for Christmas. That was now champagne money. They were going to celebrate tonight, come hell or high water. They were going to celebrate, because David was going leave that blankety-blank company if she had anything to say about it, and she had a lot to say about it because he listened to her and trusted her take on things. The sky was the limit for a man like David, as long as he didn't let the big bullies on the playground push him around.

Molly bit her lip, and then spread a glossy second coat of lipstick over the little divot her teeth left behind. She threw her red hair back over her shoulders and smoothed the wrinkles from the front of her favorite dress.

"That's okay, honey," she whispered to herself, listening to his feet plodding up the stairs, "I'll be your bull dog."

David was the best foreman they'd ever had. He'd pulled that day shift into shape when nobody else could. He worked himself ragged, put off vacation time with her and the kids, backstopped that shiftless excuse for a night manager when they needed him to, and what did he have to show for it? What? Another pass-over. Another injury on top of the insult of his paycheck, another…

"I got it," he said, unbuttoning his shirt as he entered the room.

"What?" she exclaimed. "You got it?"

"Uh-huh," he mumbled and disappeared into their bathroom.

David listened to his wife's long squeal of delight and closed the bathroom door before she could reach him with those wide open arms and their "I knew you could do it!" hug. He didn't want to be hugged right now.

He didn't want to be touched.

He turned the exhaust fan on quickly, partly to send her the message that he shouldn't be disturbed and partly to muffle all that noisy glee that came pouring through the door in question upon question about how much of a raise was he going to get, how did Al Jeffries react when he learned that David was getting the nod instead of him, and how long was it going to take him to get shaved and dressed for their first night out in months because she really felt like setting off some fireworks all over this sleepy little town. It wasn't that David begrudged her all the delight and satisfaction. He knew he had this coming. He knew they needed the money. He just didn't feel like turning handsprings, and he wasn't sure why.

Molly finally noticed he hadn't answered any of her questions, so she asked him yet another. "David? Honey, are you okay?"

"I ate something funny at lunch," he lied. "Stomach's been one big jumble ever since. Just give me a minute."

He lowered the toilet lid with the fuzzy white carpet thing on it before he sat down. Why did women put those shaggy things on the toilet lid, he wondered. Why decorate something meant for pure function? He looked around the bathroom like he'd never seen it before. Molly had decorated that bathroom within an inch of its life. No telling what she'd do with the extra money his new position would earn. She'd probably find a way to get a whirlpool crammed into this tiny water closet. Yeah. A whirlpool big enough for two.

A tiny smile cracked the stony blankness that had colonized

David's face earlier in the day. As soon as he'd heard the good news, his face had frozen. Leave it to the red-haired former cheerleader with a devilish temper and a heart of gold to thaw him out. She was so proud of him. She was so happy.

So why wasn't *he* happy?

Why wasn't *he* proud?

Molly was asking him another question, so David flushed the toilet he hadn't used and got up to shave. He ignored his reflection in the medicine cabinet mirror, while he retrieved the shaving kit and a fresh blade for the razor from its innards. He lathered up in a rush. Careful not to meet his own gaze, he concentrated on each stroke of the razor, twisting his face this way and that to facilitate the dangerous glide of soapy metal over vulnerable skin.

And then he forgot how to shave the terrain under his chin. Up? Down? Side to side? All of a sudden, he couldn't remember how to do something he'd been doing every day for twenty years.

"C'mon, stupid," he said to the man in the mirror. "Is that the best you can do?" He placed the razor alongside his Adam's apple and started it on a hesitant journey toward his dimpled chin. "Moron," he muttered, and cut himself.

He watched blood stripe the white shaving cream on his throat with red.

It didn't hurt much. That couldn't have been why he was suddenly crying.

"Idiot," he scowled at the guy in the mirror, unable to dodge those eyes any longer. "Is that the best you can do?"

"What?" Molly said from the other side of the door. "Honey, let me in."

The door wasn't locked, but in David's house a closed master bathroom door usually meant the patriarch had entered his cave for private time and didn't want to be disturbed.

So Molly knocked softly, worried all of a sudden. "David?"

"Is that the best you can do?" she heard him shout on the other side of the door. Then she heard glass breaking and began to push the bathroom door open. Damn those thick mauve throw rugs. All they did was get in the way.

71

"Stupid idiot moron!" her husband yelled at the mirror he was breaking with his shaving cream can. "Is that the best you can…?"

Molly pushed her way past the rugs and found her sweet guy with blood running down his chin and hot sweaty tears making Braveheart tracks through the shaving cream on his face. He looked at her with eyes that were far younger and yet much older than his thirty-six years. He looked at her with eyes housing both fire and rain.

Molly took the shaving cream and razor out of David's hands and checked them both for cuts.

"It's okay," he said, embarrassed. "I'm okay."

"Like hell," she said, and grabbed a bath towel in one hand and grasped one of his arms with the other. She steered him around broken shards of bathroom mirror on the floor and drew him back out into the bedroom.

"That was pretty stupid," he said, because he couldn't think of some other word for what he'd just done. He was afraid to label the outburst anything else.

Molly didn't say anything, and her silence spooked him even more.

She sat him down on the bed and wiped the shaving cream off his face. She dabbed his cut with a corner of the towel well enough to tell he hadn't slit his own throat. Then she pulled him close and let him cry and bleed all over her favorite dress. Having watched him stiff-upper-lip it through his mother's long deathbed vigil and all the way through the funeral, Molly had begun to wonder if he'd ever get to the tears.

Who would have thought her mild-mannered prince would have to get angry first? He cried for something close to twenty minutes—way past their dinner reservation, that's for sure. When he had himself together again, he said he wished his mother had lived long enough to see him get the promotion.

"I wish she could've seen me pull this off, you know?"

Molly bit her lip again to keep from saying something David didn't seem ready to hear. She even felt a little guilty for thinking uncharitably of the deceased.

72

The old lady was gone, after all. What did it matter if history got rewritten with a forgiving and forgetful pen? Molly would probably want her kids to forget all the little and big mistakes she was making while trying her best to raise them well. So what if David was burying the bad along with the good his mother had done? She'd been a widow for decades, raising David alone, demanding perfection from herself *and* her eleven-year-old boy. She had been tough as nails for both their sakes.

Molly kissed her husband's hair and mopped up his face. She ordered an everything-on-it pizza while David took a shower and finished the shave. They put on their pajamas. He built a fire in the fireplace they hardly ever used. They had a child-free night ahead of them, and Molly was more determined than ever to make the very best of it. When the pizza arrived, David surprised her by pulling a bottle of champagne out of the ice maker in the freezer. He had picked it up on the way home from work. He popped the cork with a grin.

"We can launch some fireworks right here at home," he winked at her.

"We most definitely can," she said.

David dug out their wine glasses and toasted his wife for choosing him instead of one of the guys who could have given her the grand life she deserved.

"What are you talking about?" she asked. "Who said…?"

"This is as good as it gets for me, Molly."

"David…"

"This is the best I can do."

"That's not you talking."

"It's the truth."

"No, David Michael O'Brien, it is *not* the truth. But it is—to the letter—exactly what your mother said to you every Thanksgiving we spent with her. Her house or our house, didn't make any difference. She always said the same thing."

David's face had become a stony blank again.

"You've wiped it out of your mind, haven't you?" she asked.

He had. Molly set down her champagne and put her arms

around him.

"She'd watch you carve up the turkey…"

David's mouth opened.

"You'd set off carving it this way or that, and she'd start frowning. Who cares how the bloomin' turkey gets hacked up anyway. Your *father'd* been the butcher, not you. But you'd do your best. You'd give everybody but *yourself* their favorite piece of the bird. And she'd sit there and watch and wait until you sat down to eat, and then she'd say 'Is that the best you can do?' Every other word for the rest of the night was about how you couldn't do this and you couldn't do that and how you weren't ever going to amount to…"

David placed two fingers over his wife's lips.

"Sorry," she whispered.

David was sorry, too. But he was also glad she had brought it all back to him.

Now he could start to mourn the *other* mother he'd buried a month ago.

The mother who *admired* the way her son cut up Thanksgiving's main course.

The mother who could respect a hard-earned C+ instead of dubbing her son "a stupid moron."

The mother who would have revered hard work and an even temper more than a big bank roll and cruel clout.

The mother David had always wanted, and now would never ever have.

And one day—when the fresh ache of this loss was behind him—David would finally mourn the father who wasn't there to teach him a proper way to shave.

THEY NEVER STOP BEING YOUR PARENTS
Patricia's Story

Light. Everywhere.

That was the first thing that threw her off. Patricia expected it to be dark. That's how it used to be. She was counting on the darkness. She had anticipated finding comfort and strength in the shadows and expected to feel consoled by that dim, yellow glow spilling through the small square of dense mesh.

But this was a room, not a confessional. It even had a window, for God's sake, and cream-colored walls. There was carpet on the floor and a partition she could have easily stepped around to meet the priest face to face. It even smelled different—like freesia potpourri or one of her aromatic candles. No stale odor of incense and stagnant holy water. Nothing dank or musty about it. A padded chair beckoned her to sit eyeball to eyeball with her confessor.

They had to be kidding. Patricia could never tell the old priest off, face to face. The message she came to deliver could only be uttered if he couldn't see her and she didn't have to look at him. She had needed to fortify herself with wine even to pull off a *veiled* confrontation. If the priest could see the assault coming, she might lose her nerve completely. Spouting the truth about her father after all these decades of silence was not going to be easy. She'd choose the kneeler and the screen, thank you.

In her fantasies, Patricia had seen herself marching into the rectory right after the funeral and confronting the pastor with all the rage she felt but couldn't express until her father was dead and cold in his grave. All during the wake, the funeral, the burial—she kept dreaming of this moment. Her palms were moist with anticipation of it. Her head was spinning with all that she would say, all the secrets she would tell. But as the day had worn on, Patricia had begun to feel oppressed by all the pomp and circumstance. She felt flocked in by her mother and brother, her aunts and uncles. She was surrounded by enablers and codependents—all her father's family, friends and co-workers who knew the man they were burying as the exemplary employee, the loyal Knight of Columbus, the usher with the kindest smile, the most reliable brother's keeper, the model husband…and perfect father.

Their illusions drained her strength, crippled her resolve.

Patricia realized she could never spill the nasty beans in the pastor's office where the priest's black suit and white collar would make him seem all powerful, where he could pose as someone who knew her father better than she had, where he would appear so pure and righteous that Patricia would only feel all the more dirty and wrong. Besides, he would recognize her immediately and probably head off the attack with a litany of condolences and consolations. Or worse, he might silence her with an incredulous frown, calling her a liar and an ungrateful daughter.

She had slept fitfully last night, until it dawned on her that there was another way to bring the truth to light. After the solution came to her, she slept like a baby, in spite of all the memories that had swirled around her the moment she stepped back into the family house where so much in her young life had gone so wrong.

In the confessional, the priest's sole purpose was to listen, and he—at least—was going to hear what kind of a man her father had been. At long, long last, Patricia would get to do all the talking. No one would silence her. No one would interrupt. She just had to lure the priest in, soften him up by pretending to be sorry for her sins, asking for absolution. Then she would launch a sneak attack, just like he'd blasted her with all those glowing accolades and kudos for a monster. Now it was her turn, and Patricia planned to blindside the righteous reverend with truth, the way he had ambushed her with lies.

All the daylight and openness of the re-decorated "confessional" tried to undermine her dark purpose, but Patricia wasn't falling for it. She'd rehearsed this scene far too long and too well to have it rewritten by the attractive trimmings of some "Sacrament of Reconciliation." Reconciliation. What a joke.

Patricia remained hidden on the faceless side of the partition and lowered her rusty, middle-aged knees onto the leather cushion.

She had not meant to make the Sign of the Cross. That was the second thing to catch her by surprise. Her hand operated on automatic, doing that devout dance from brow to heart and shoulder to shoulder.

"Forgive me, Father, for I have sinned," she said, and struggled to regain her unholy purpose in spite of the blessing he mumbled at her. Thrown off by her own self-inflicted sign of devotion, Patricia stumbled. Now that she had him right where she wanted him, paying attention, leaning toward her—oh, yes, she could hear him breathing on the other side of the little mesh square—now that her big moment had arrived, she couldn't see just how to let the sordid little cat out of its scummy bag.

Nor could she remember what she was supposed to say next.

"How long has it been since your last confession?" the priest prompted her.

His voice sounded different from yesterday. Not quite as sanctimonious, not quite so above it all. Patricia figured this warm, helpful tone was a priest's equivalent of the physician's "bedside manner," the reassuring bait they laid for all the poor suckers who traipsed in week after week, pouring out their guts, hoping for something to wash their tarry sins away.

"Excuse me?" the priest said. "How long did you say it's been?"

Patricia had mumbled her answer the first time and was angry that she had to speak up. "About thirty years, I said."

He whistled. Whistled! And then he said, "That's a good long while."

"Is that a problem?" she asked.

Why on earth hadn't she lied?

"Well. A problem for *whom*?"

"For *you*," she said, "Is there some kind of time limit, some sort of deadline I've missed?" she asked.

"No, no deadline," he said. "I was just wondering why."

"Why what? Why it's been so long, or why I'm here now?"

"Both actually."

Patricia couldn't help chuckling. He was playing into her hand now.

"What's so funny?" he asked.

"Nothing. Nothing is the least bit funny. I could give you the same answer to both questions, that's all."

"And that answer would be...?"

"You sound like a reasonably intelligent man, Father," she said, deciding to play with him for a while. "Maybe you'll be able to figure it out."

"I see. You want me to solve a riddle."

"What riddle?" asked Patricia.

"The riddle of why you're here after thirty years about to confess a ton of sins for which you aren't the least bit sorry."

Patricia was speechless.

He was trying to spoil her fun. It was as if he could see what she was up to and was trying to head her off at the pass. Maybe he knew who she was, after all. Maybe he could see her through the mesh and was being cryptic because he'd noticed that hers was the only dry eye rimming the graveside. He'd been paying attention yesterday, and this was payback for disrespecting the parish's fallen hero. This was the terse tone a good pastor reserved for hardened hearts who buried parents without shedding a tear while their eyes screamed: "Good riddance! Good riddance to bad rubbish!"

Patricia squinted as hard as she could but still couldn't see more than a dim outline of the priest on the other side. So unless he had x-ray vision, her identity was still a secret. For a moment, she thought he might have recognized her voice, but how could that be? She'd barely spoken three words to him: a curt, little "Hello" when her mother introduced them and the entirely insincere "Thank you, Father" she shoved out between her lips at the end of the service yesterday. No, he couldn't have known her by voice, and he couldn't see her. Yet he seemed to have peeped her hole card, nonetheless.

Not sorry for her sins....

How could he have known that?

Well, the only way to get back the advantage was to launch her assault early as opposed to late in the game. The best defense was, after all....

"Frankly, Father," she said, "I didn't come here to talk about why I've been away from the Church. I came here to make peace with God," she lied. "I came here hoping to reconcile myself to Him. With all due respect, who are you to say I'm not sorry for my sins?" she asked, allowing herself to sound wounded. "Is this how the Church welcomes back one of its lost sheep?"

The priest filled the uncomfortable silence between them with a deep sigh.

Patricia smiled. She'd shamed him back into his place. Now she could get on with it. First, she'd confess to a long list of sordid transgressions. That wouldn't be hard. She wouldn't have to make any of them up either. Oh, Patricia would drench him with her wickedness! The old priest would have to sit there while she tarred his virgin ears with filth. And then she'd finger one of the most beloved among his flock as being the inspiration for all her misdeeds, the architect of her corruption, the vandal who plundered her innocence when she was only...

"Ten," said the voice on the other side of the partition. "You were ten, Patty."

"How?" Patricia gasped. "How...do...you...know?"

A man's hand pressed against the mesh, so close to her face Patricia could feel its body heat. The huge hand wore a wedding ring.

"I am so sorry, honey," that too-familiar voice said.

"Oh, no," Patricia sobbed. "Daddy."

Her legs turned to mushy lead like they always did whenever she had one of these dreams about her father and tried to run away. But this time, she made her legs work, made them lift her up off the kneeler. This time she meant to escape.

"I'm so sorry," she heard her father say again.

Patricia swam her way through fear-thickened air, stumbling backwards toward the door. The nightmare turned everything dark. She broke out in a sweat.

"Forgive me, Patty," he was begging her, and she could hear him rising from his seat on the other side of the screen.

He had never asked her for forgiveness, not in scores upon scores of nightmares—and never ever face to face. Why now?

"Forgive me please."

What was this? His spirit's fearful dodge of judgement?

"No!" Patricia cried, grappling for the door's tiny knob, "It's too late!"

"Honey, baby.... "

His shadow on the wall moved closer.

"Daddy's so sorry."

* * * * * * *

Patricia bolted up in bed, gasping for air, choking down her sobs.

She pulled her mind out of the nightmare and waited for her heart to stop trying to pound its way out of her chest. Why had she ever agreed to stay under her mother's roof, in the bedroom of her childhood where so many sins had been committed—none of them hers. Why had she even returned for the funeral?

Her nightgown and linens were soaked through with sweat and..."Oh, God," she whispered, realizing she'd wet the bed.

Just like old times.

A rainstorm masked the watery whir of her shower, its thunder and lightning subpoenaed witnesses to her shame. Patricia tied the wet sheets and nightgown in a bundle and made the bed up again, even though the mattress was damp.

She dressed quickly and quietly, trying hard not to think, not to remember, and for God's sake not to feel. She packed her suitcase and used her cellphone to call a taxi. Her shoeless feet tiptoed downstairs, past the living room full of flowers, past her brother snoring on the sofa.

She put her pumps on while standing in the foyer by the front door, and then she hesitated, feeling as though she should at least leave her mother a note.

But what would she say? What could she possibly say?

Easing the front door closed behind her, Patricia stood on the stoop and let tears mix with the rain on her face. Dry-eyed at his funeral, she let them flow now, for *herself*. She dropped her bundle of soiled sheets in the trash can at the corner and hailed the next taxi that drove by—whether or not it was the one she had called.

She left her father's ghost behind to work out its own salvation and spent the rest of the night at the airport, counting down the hours until the next flight out.

Meditation

I remember one funeral where the father of eleven was being eulogized by the eldest son. His words were filled with admiration and warmth, which was somewhat surprising since that father had left the family after getting sober with the help of Alcoholics Anonymous. The abandoned family seemed to me to be amazingly forgiving, at least until the son sat down. Then, unannounced, he was followed by an irate brother who took back all that the older sibling had said. Which, in turn, caused a defending daughter to offer her own counterpoint, followed by another rebuttal by her sister. There were seven testimonies in all, each spilling over with grief, anger, love and disappointment. That day, the funeral service went much longer than was planned and revealed much more than was probably necessary.

Our parents bring out the best and worst in us, in death as in life. Sometimes our relationship with them was not what we wanted it to be...or what it should have been if life were fair. Sometimes we are angry or disappointed with the parent who died or the one who remains alive. The wake and funeral might—as in the case of Richard, David and Patricia—just bring everything to a head.

Certainly, some parents have done a poor job raising their kids—some from ignorance, some from lack of skill or resources, some from mean-spiritedness or downright cussedness. Their death means all that is over. Now the forgiveness must begin. Now comes the resurrection after death. Now the salvation follows the suffering. All that is left for their children is to decide how to reconcile themselves to the reality that was their mom or dad. Sometimes that takes another lifetime.

WK

Get on with Your Life

You've buried one of the giants in your world—your mother or your father, or both together (in what must be one of the greatest tragedies human beings are asked to endure). Their departure was either a surprise or sadly expected. Your experience of their exit was either up close and personal or distant. Either you were a featured player in what preceded and followed their death, or you got the news over the phone and had to travel from far away to see for yourself that the inconceivable was indeed true. Maybe your relationship with your parent was healthy and warm, or perhaps it was a bond far less comforting. The goodbye may have been tender and transcendent, or perhaps it was chilly and full of regret.

In one sense, it doesn't matter which variation of the above applies to you personally. The fact is, your mother or father is gone. Yet, everything else in your life is to a large extent just where you left it. The load at work is just as heavy, the kids are just as rambunctious, the bills are piled just as high (and maybe even higher). The sun still shines, rain still falls, gravity still works, and none of the forces of nature seem to care one bit that your personal universe has been altered forever.

How can that be? How can everyone you encounter expect you to accept that all is as it should be, that this fresh and gaping wound of yours is part of life? How can they tell you to get over it after a month or even just a couple weeks of grieving?

Many cultures have gracious traditions of mourning built into their social customs. But here in our society there is no set of rituals that allows people to hang their head after the funeral, no such thing as formal bereavement leave from our responsibilities.

Maybe there should be.

REMINDED OF YOUR OWN MORTALITY
Marty's Story

Tonight, twenty years of struggle pay off for Marty Enders, big time.

Cable television is crowning him King of Comedy for the two decades he's spent broiling television's alternative airwaves with the most astute, political humor since Mort Sahl made 'em wince. His pal Billy Crystal heads an impressive line-up of comics, each of whom were happy to stop through Vegas if it meant they could roast Marty alive. Crystal delivers a Freudian upper cut to Marty's ever-present cigar. Then comes a quick jab to the Jewish heritage, followed by a Robin Williams roundhouse hammering Marty's joke-writing for a certain former president, who "Let's just say, shares Marty's love for Cuban contraband."

At last, the victim can respond, and he's brilliant—never funnier, the cigar delicately punctuating the driest of wits. He loses himself in the waves of laughter rolling through his audience, all the pretty ladies and prosperous gentlemen chortling into their drinks.

And then he loses his train of thought.

Mid-anecdote, the punch-line evaporates. A nervous draw on his cigar, and every joke he's ever told dissolves into oblivion. "I'm so up it feels like down to me," he quips, a shiny moustache of sweat misting over his upper lip.

Crystal helps him out like the pro and the friend he is by jump-starting the standing ovation. But the vital forty-five-year-old taking the bows feels much too young for this Alzheimer's act.

At the party afterwards, he wants his wife Esther close by his side. This love of the past twenty-five years knows something is wrong when—in the middle of introducing her to "They call me *Mister* Cosby!"—Marty draws another blank and forgets her name.

It's obvious to Esther that her husband is over tired and over committed, stretched to the limit after a month spent on the road trying out new material for his next HBO special. There's a hosting gig for "Saturday Night Live" in the works, with Leno sandwiched somehow in between.

"But this booby-trapped memory is the worst," Marty tells his wife.

Esther wants him to stay home for a while. She reminds him that this is the last weekend he can see their teenaged son's performance as Horatio in his high school's production of "Hamlet."

Marty promises he'll try his best to be there, but he's got this show biz race to run while the running is good. He's gotta keep the pedal to the floor while his foot can still find it.

Esther listens sympathetically, looking both bemused and befuddled. Her guess is that Marty's not sure just where he's racing. Underneath his exhaustion, there's some kind of itch he can't seem to scratch.

His big night passes full of laughs and affection from friends, but later at home Esther feels him tossing sleeplessly beside her in bed. He gets up, lights a cigar, puts it out, looks in on his son, and paces the living room. She finds him watching Nick at Night's old Dick Van Dyke shows and leads him back into the bedroom. She's opened their drapes to the desert sunrise, so glad they traded the maddening crowd in Malibu for the peaceful retirement rhythms of the high desert. Their view of empty Nevada is the backdrop for a talk about the future.

"What do I do with the next forty-five years?" Marty wonders.

Esther doesn't have the answers, but it's reassuring lying close to her like this. He kisses her and is making moves for more, when desire is conquered by sleep.

* * * * * *

Unfortunately, Marty has forgotten about the car his assistant has arranged to pick him up at six the next morning, so he can ride to the airport, catch a plane, and wing west to Los Angeles for a round robin of hi-and-howdys, meetings and HBO's hastily scheduled appearance on "The Tonight Show." Usually Esther reminds him of these things, but Marty failed to tell her about this trip, because he forgot he promised his manager he'd take it. So with his wife's help Marty throws some clothes in a suitcase, jumps in the car, and just makes his flight.

His temporary home: the Beverly-Wilshire Hotel.

The name of this game: Busy, busy, busy. Run, run, run.

After meetings with network execs on the CBS lot and movie producers in Burbank—a weary Marty is greeted at the hotel by a lobby full of hellos from friends, plus a message to call Esther ASAP. He phones her from his suite, but his son tells him she's out. The boy has his fingers crossed, hoping Dad won't miss his last night as Horatio.

"Not for the world," Marty promises. "I'll be home tomorrow noon."

"Yeah, right," is all the hope this teen can muster. He's heard that one before.

Marty hangs up having forgotten to ask his son why Esther called. He decides to ring her up on her cellphone, but can't remember the number! He calls home again, hoping Rafael has it handy, only to discover his son has ducked out as well.

"If I only had a brain!" Marty sighs, and lays back on the bed, hoping a nap will prevent him from taking this absent-minded professor act nationwide via Leno's show. A call from the limousine driver waiting downstairs in the hotel lobby is all that wakes him up in time to dress for the show.

He bolts a drink in the Green Room before facing the Leno audience. Thank God, Marty's funny. He even remembers to plug the HBO thing, but forgets all about "Saturday Night Live." So, Jay has to shill for the network.

During the commercial break, Marty apologizes.

"Forget it," Jay assures him, but can't help noticing, "you look tired, Marty."

A moody ride back to the hotel ends with a surprise awaiting him in his room. Esther has flown in, with good news and bad news.

Marty wants the bad news first.

She tells him he has to cancel every appointment he's set up for tomorrow.

"And the good news?"

"I am here to make sure you will not disappoint our son again."

"But I have to…"

"Nor will you break your mother's heart by missing the unveiling of your father's headstone tomorrow morning."

"Oh. Oh, my."

"I know. You forgot."

* * * * * *

Marty's mother looks perfectly serene and beautiful, admiring the stone she's had chiseled and laid in place for her husband. The two doves hovering together in the granite anticipate her name joining his one day. The plot has space enough to accommodate her eventual arrival. But there is nothing morbid about the brief ceremony, nothing burdensome about her hand on Marty's arm.

He is the one with the dark cloud on his shoulders. He is the one trying to dodge a disquieting truth.

After recitation of the Yizkor, Esther and friends of the family place their pebbles on the headstone. Then they leave mother and son alone for a while.

"So, what's with this senility act?" his mother asks out of the blue.

"What are you talkin' about?" says Marty. She always put him on the defensive.

"You think I'm blind, I can't watch television?" she says. "I'm so poor, I don't get cable? Please."

"You saw the roast-thing."

"Me and Hilda watched Billy Crystal pull your chestnuts out of the fire."

"Geez, Louise."

"That's why he's doin' the Oscars, and you're not."

"He's not doin' the Oscars anymore, Ma."

"If Billy'd been on Leno, he could've saved your chestnuts twice in one week."

"I didn't bomb on Leno, Ma."

"I could've driven a truck through every joke."

"I did not forget my lines on Leno, Ma."

"But you were *afraid* you would. Weren't you?"

The half a hug he gives her is answer enough.

She tugs at his coat sleeve. "Come on, let's get out of here. The old guy's not gettin' back up."

As they make their way toward the others, Marty comes clean, "I don't know what's happening, Ma. It's all I can do to remember my name half the time."

"Tell me about it. My life's one long 'senior moment.'"

"With all due respect, I don't think forty-five years make me a 'senior.'"

"No?"

"I don't get those discounts at the movies."

"And you want I should feel sorry for you? That's one of the few perks comin' my way these days, kid."

Marty cracks his first smile in twenty-four hours.

"Of course your *father* could learn a sketch or a routine in one afternoon and have it perfect for life."

"Thanks, Ma, that's just what I needed to hear."

"Do you remember your very first laugh, Marty?"

"My first laugh when?"

She stops them in the middle of the path, still yards from the others, and forty years drop off her face. Her memory of her son's first laugh is that fresh and sweet.

"You were six years old. I sneaked you backstage during one of your father's routines. He was still working with Max then, may they both rest in peace now, and the sketch called for your father to 'die' and then wake up and surprise the undertaker. You had to be there. Anyway, that man, your father, croaked with all the dignity of a king. You'd have thought he was playing Lear on the Great White Way, not mining laughs in some rundown vaudeville house. So, he's out there on stage moaning like his life's really coming to an end. I mean, the man was inches away from getting booed off the stage, but you saved the day."

"Me?"

"You might have been afraid to watch him die, I think, 'cause you were whimpering so loud I was afraid the audience was gonna hear. And all of a sudden you yell out, 'Daddy, Daddy, wipe your nose!'"

"Oh, great. Pop must've really appreciated that."

"He *did*. You stole the show, the audience fell out of their seats, and you were hooked on show biz for life."

"So, that was my first laugh."

"And one of the last for Maximillian and Enders."

His mother's ready to sit down and steers them on toward the limousines.

"How come?" Marty asks.

"Vaudeville was just about history anyway, but then Max died a month after that. Heart attack took him out like that."

She snaps her fingers and, even with her arthritis, the pop seems to echo.

Marty remembers really missing his "Uncle Max." "That must've been the first time I realized people could leave and not come back."

"Yep."

"Max had to be pretty young for a heart attack."

"What's young?" she shrugs. "He was forty-five. Like you."

"Like me," he says, with a glance back toward his father's resting place. His mother has tripped over the one truth Marty Enders would most like to forget.

"Ah, so that's what's bothering you," she says. "Life is a play with a death scene in the last act, Marty. Accept it, get ready for it, and then forget about it."

"Forget about it?"

Another shrug, "Why not? What good's it do to worry? Taking my cue from Max and your father, I'm thinking death comes as the ultimate surprise."

* * * * * *

That night, Marty's son does a sweet job sending Hamlet's spirit on its way: "*Good night, sweet prince, and flights of angels sing thee to thy rest!*"

GET UP, GET OVER IT
Beth's Story

"Sorry for your loss, Ms. Webster."

"Thank you, Kenny."

"Good to see you back, Beth."

"Good to be back, Joanne."

"Sorry about your Dad, Beth."

"Thanks, Virginia."

"Lost my mom last year, you know."

"No, I didn't know. I'm so sorry."

"Hey, Beth, how's my favorite sales director?"

"I'm the only sales director, Gary, least I was when I left."

"You doin' okay, kid?"

"I'm fine. Sandra tells me you've been holding down the fort."

"I got your back, that's for sure."

"Ah, so that explains the knife I found sticking out of it."

"What are you talking about?"

"I want to see you in my office in fifteen."

"I have a meeting with…"

"Me, in fifteen minutes."

"But Bob and I are…"

"Both meeting with me in fifteen minutes."

Beth closed the outer office door behind her and heaved a sigh of relief.

Her secretary, Sandra, didn't even look up from her computer screen. "Told you on the phone you should wait 'til Monday."

"I know," said Beth, taking the messages out of Sandra's hand.

"You should've given yourself the weekend."

"I thought I could sneak in and read some mail."

"Didn't I just hear you set a meeting with the piranha and the shark?"

"Keep your friends close, keep your enemies closer."

"That must be some more of that gospel according to Sun Tzu you keep quoting," said Sandra, following Beth into her inner office, "'cause even though the good Lord said, 'Love your enemies,' he didn't say squat about holdin' 'em close."

"Close but not too close," said Beth.

"Whatever." Sandra watched her boss drop her briefcase and newspaper on the visitor's sofa. "Are you sure you're going to be able to tell friend from foe, Chief?"

"Let's hope."

"Lot of musical chairs got played while you were gone."

Beth opened the door to her office and gasped at the piles of paper on her desk. "Oh, my God," she said, seriously considering an about-face.

"You wanted to see the full load. I separated mail from memos. Personal from business. Right-away from this-can-wait. There are post-its on everything."

"Okay, okay, let me ease into this," Beth said, hanging up her coat. "Take the memos, leave the mail. Take the this-can-wait, leave the right-away."

"Got it."

"And hold all calls for an hour."

"Sure thing," said Sandra, gathering up two of the piles. "I probably shouldn't ask this, but how we doin' on the caffeine fast?"

"Better give me a shot."

"You sure?"

"Between you and me, I'm not too almighty sure of anything just now."

"I'll make it half decaf."

"Sounds good. When piranha and shark get here…"

"Yep?"

"Pretend I'm on the phone, huh? Make 'em wait a little while."

"I'd love to."

"Thanks."

"Pleasure's mine."

"Oh, and thank you for the bonsai. It's stunning."

"That was from everybody, honey."

"The card, sure. No way this company gives a bonsai for condolences."

"I know you like them," said Sandra. "Besides, all flowers do is wither and die. Who the hell needs that at a time like this? They say bonsai can have longer life spans than most humans."

"I just pray I don't kill it."

"Give it the time and attention it needs, and it'll do just fine."

"Yes, ma'am, I catch your drift," said Beth, easing herself behind the desk.

Sandra did an about-face in the doorway, her face softer than usual. "I have a confession to make, Chief."

"Is that right?"

"You remember that party you had at your place about a year or so back, while your dad was in town?"

Beth's face heated up with the memory, "Wow, I'd forgotten about that. That was a great evening."

"Yes, it was. I wanted you to know how much it meant that you invited me. You certainly didn't have to."

"I wanted you to meet him."

"I'm glad you did. We talked a good long while, him and me."

"I remember you two huddling on the sofa for a while. He was full of questions about my job after that."

"We weren't just talking about *you*, you know," said Sandra.

Her tone forced the younger woman to assess her secretary by an altogether different standard. Suddenly, Sandra's age and widowed eligibility, her well preserved figure and loyal-to-the-core character had a totally new and charming dimension. Her father had been a very debonair widower himself for years before his death. "That was one fine man, my dear," said Sandra. "*Very* charming."

"Yes," Beth said carefully, "he most certainly was."

"Hard to think that much charisma could ever give up the ghost."

"Why, Sandra, did you have a crush on my old man?" asked Beth with a little laugh attached to make the truth easier on both of them.

93

The sad ring around Sandra's smile was all the answer she gave. Beth nodded. "Well, I guess we should all just get in line and take a number."

Sandra heaved a sigh and offered one last tender piece of advice on her way out. "Steady as she goes in here today, all right?"

"All right."

But the nosebleed-high view out Beth's window proved more compelling than anything on her desk. All her thoughts were labeled Dad and saturated with grief.

After she'd counted the number of floors under construction on the high-rise across the street…after she'd watched a chopper settle over the white-X landing pod of another…after she'd studied the numbers painted on top of five city buses, dividing them by three, four, five…

Her intercom buzzed, but Beth didn't answer the first summons.

She placed a section of her newspaper on top of each pile of paper, stacked the piles one on top of another, and then buried them under her desk out of sight. Wouldn't do for Piranha and Shark to see her buried under responsibilities she had yet to meet. She checked her face in her compact's mirror to make sure she had on her game face, then she pushed Sandra's com-line button.

"Send them in," she said.

"Right away," said Sandra.

Beth stood up, and turned her gaze out the window again so that her back would face the door. She folded her arms across her chest, focused on the boat with the whitest, fullest sail, and repeated her new mantra, "Steady as she goes."

Meditation

The work of grieving the loss of a parent is jolting and exhausting. Our more assertive friends give us countermanding advice: On the one hand we are to "take time" for ourselves and on the other we are to "get over it" as quickly as possible. Our more sensitive friends give us a wide berth, respecting our feelings even to the point of absenting themselves from our lives—at a time when we might need them the most.

Marty and Beth have to arrive at what Elisabeth Kubler-Ross called "the stage of acceptance." But the acceptance of the death of our parents is also the acceptance of our own mortality. When we reach that acceptance, our grief is not over but has run like a river into a great reservoir of sadness that is part of the water table of every soul. Somehow we all float on that reservoir, only occasionally dipping into it. The floating is what we call "getting on with life."

So how do we get on with our life? Time, of course, heals—but ever so slowly. Being busy helps—but sometimes this only masks our pain. Here is another time-honored source of overcoming our grief: Go deeper into the reservoir of human sadness and touch the pain of others. John Shea tells a wonderful story about a grieving woman who goes to a spiritual master for comfort. The holy man agrees to counsel her, but he asks that she first go to the homes surrounding them and collect sticks for a fire. "But only take wood from a house that has lost no one," the master says. The woman comes back many hours later—without any wood, but with her grief healed.

WK

95

Now Who Am I?

Most probably, your parents are the two people you have known the longest. Depending on how old they were when you were born and how old they are when they die, you may have known them most of their adult lives. Perhaps you knew them in their twenties and thirties on into their sixties and seventies. You've been witness to a large part of their lifetime. You saw who they were, or at least who they seemed to be to you. You saw who they became, and who they were when they left this world.

And now their life has ended.

Yet your life goes on without them, as changed by their absence as it was influenced by their presence.

What are you going to do now?

Who are you going to be now that they are no longer watching and advising, ignoring or deriding—at least not in the same manner they employed before?

Any changes afoot in your life, besides the ones that cause rivers of tears and flash floods of memories?

Any urge to forgive rising up out of rage?

Any healing of old wounds inviting you to try them on?

Any new insights pouring in over the loss?

Are any fresh winds blowing through your corner of the universe?

Have any new adventures called to you from afar?

FORGIVE BUT DON'T FORGET
Delle's Story

Good morning, Mom

I have your picture, my favorite picture of you, sitting on the windowsill of my kitchen, but it won't stay there long. Don't want to make the same mistake Dad did with his favorite picture of me and leave it where the sun can bleach the color out. But a day or two shouldn't hurt, and your back is to the sun.

Your face is turned toward me. What a beauty God has with him now, Mom. What a knockout. I don't think I ever told you how pretty I thought you were. That made us even, I guess, 'cause you never told me either. And now....

I've been thinking about you a lot, of course. But these thoughts are different. *I'm* different. Your dying changed me. The woman you let me get to know in those last weeks changed who I am and who I can now be.

I may renovate Delle using a few pieces of Joyce you finally let me see.

Think I'll lay claim to that droll humor you used to season the hospital food. Sure wish the rest of us comedians at home had let you get in a joke now and then while I was growing up. We buried your subtle wit with broad hilarity.

I may also find some use for the humility you developed in regard to your physical appearance. It was more comfortable than all that brittle, intimidating vanity you employed to hold me and the world at a distance.

I was moved by your reverent desire for Communion after going so many years without receiving it. My duties as a Eucharistic minister will be all the sweeter forever more.

I'm grateful that—out of all the family members present to hear them—I was the one who understood the wisps of Scripture you sighed into the air occasionally. I felt privileged to realize the Baptist-turned-Catholic that you were had memorized so much of the Good Book before your conversion. I felt blessed to recognize how Proverbs and Philippians were weaving coded messages that revealed your readiness to leave this world for the next. It was like sharing a holy secret with you, Mom. And it's made me love the Bible even more.

Most of all, Mom, I want to inherit your utter conviction that Jesus stood waiting for your soul on the other side of the final surrender.

"I want to get up out of this bed," you said, gasping for air during a treatment. "I want to stand up on my feet and say 'Come on, Jesus, I'm ready, let's go!'"

I wish I could know you all over again, Mom. In this precious early morning moment, I wish I were eighteen years old again, so we could be friends for decades longer—better friends than ever before.

One of the moments I want to share at your service next week is that last big hug we had while I was helping the nurse change your bed.

Do you, can you, remember?

I scooped the top half of you into my arms and told you to put your arm around my neck, which you did, and I lifted you into my arms for a long embrace in the middle of the move. You were so tiny, so light.

"I got you, Mom," I said.

"You got me," you said.

"How's this for a hug, huh? Doesn't it feel good?"

"Yes," you said.

"Do you know how many hugs I have stored up for you? Do you?" I whispered into your ear. "Hundreds. How come you only let me give you so few of them?"

You didn't answer.

You didn't have to.

I think you were wondering why yourself.

I love you, Mom.

I forgive you for all the hugs we didn't share, all those hugs you said I didn't need. I give them to you now. Can you feel them? Oh, how I hope so.

Your daughter always,
Delle

WILL THE REAL ME PLEASE STAND UP?
Frank's Story

"Well, this has been a real pleasure."

"Thanks. Same here."

"Honestly, we were surprised the 'Killer Litigator' agreed to meet with us."

Frank tried hard not to roll his eyes when the idiot used his media nickname. Only his ex-wife had dared to use it in his presence. And she, at least, had known it was no compliment.

"Well, we're just launching this firm, you know, and, yeah, the three of us have got decent pedigree, but you're Frank Wolf, for crying out loud."

"People still talk about Behr and Behr's meltdown after you left."

"Behr, Sr.'s retirement was the real loss, not me."

"Most people think he retired because you left him alone with Junior."

Frank shrugged. It was a weak response but he didn't have a stronger one. He wanted the interview to end without their inviting him to lunch and without his having to answer The Question.

"You've still got to meet with our third musketeer, of course," said Lutterman.

"He'll be back in town on Monday," said Redding.

"Right, and we can start hammering out the offer then. But the two of us think the law firm of Lutterman, Redding and Cole would be damn lucky to have you at any price."

"That's great," said Frank, getting to his feet.

"We've just got one more question before we let you go."

Frank felt his stomach muscles tighten. He sat back down. His mind spun thirty seconds into the future, searching for an answer to The Question he knew was coming. "Fire away."

"Why the year and a half off?"

"After you left Behr and Behr?"

They waited a moment, but Frank didn't have an answer ready yet.

"We understand your taking the time off to care for your father."

"That was really first class."

"But Jim'll ask about the gap since the funeral. We just want to know what to tell him."

Frank nodded, but said nothing. He was trying to guess how old these two guys were. How long would it be before they started burying their parents and uncles and aunts? How long would it be before they saw the topography of their lives altered beyond recognition and found themselves unable to take the same old roads to the same old destinations because all the landmarks had changed? How long before they, too, would start having to fabricate glib, bankable answers to intensely personal questions?

"So, what'd you do after your dad, you know…? Did you do some *pro bono* that's not on the res? Travel maybe?"

"Sail around the world? That's what I'd love to do one of these days."

"Really?" asked Frank. "Then you should do it sooner than later."

Now they *knew* he was stalling. They watched him run a hand through his thinning hair, and it was their turn to "guesstimate" *his* age, one missing strand at a time. Frank could read their calculations in narrowing gazes and slightly raised eyebrows. He decided to tell them the truth. "You'll laugh," he warned them.

They promised they wouldn't, but they did, of course.

Softly. After he left the office.

* * * * * *

Killer Litigator Frank Wolf stood on the sidewalk outside the skyscraping edifice and looked up at its sleek glass and metal perfection. He definitely would not be working for Lutterman, Redding and Cole. After Lutterman and Redding finished telling Cole about Frank's new, absorbing "hobby," he would no longer be considered the prime partner material they had dubbed him a mere ten minutes ago. He'd be a freaky failure—a loony, laughing stock among those whose respect he'd courted diligently all his life, at least up until two years ago. He loosened his tie and tried hard to remember where the nearest commuter station was. A couple of years ago, his wingtips would have carried him there without his brain having to direct them.

Settling into his window seat on the train, he was glad to have beaten the work-weary crush of commuters by at least an hour. Leaving the city before three guaranteed him a spot on the left hand side of the train, the side that would face south as they chugged west toward the burbs. Today it seemed more important than usual that he have that southern view.

Frank propped his sleek valise on his lap and stared at its perfectly maintained leather and un-bruised brass fasteners. He blocked out the people around him and ignored the view outside his window until trees and grass replaced the skyscrapers and cement, ushering him beyond the city limits, delivering him safe and sound back to hicksville. He studied his hands, admiring the fresh manicure he'd endured to obliterate all evidence of his new job of choice—the new career path that inspired choked-back chortles at Lutterman, Redding and Cole.

As long as the city's castles of power and commerce rose up alongside the tracks, reminding Frank of all that he once was and hoped he might be again, the guilt in his belly marched around in circles, stomping down the relief that was also residing there. The interview replayed its last moments for him, trying to resolve the internal combat between guilt and relief one way or the other.

On the ride into town this morning, the Killer Litigator had celebrated his comeback. In his fantasies, he began spending all that big money again. His eyes scoped out the new high-rise properties popping up just inside the Loop—old lofts transformed into hot properties with the best views and amenities. He kicked himself for selling his riverfront condo two years ago and moving into his parents' old place. What was he thinking? That hadn't been necessary.

His father would have been horrified to know the family's "best and brightest" had abdicated his princely throne in the city for the sake of a dying old man who couldn't even remember who he was—or who he'd been. Frank imagined his father standing at heaven's gate, shaking his fist at his son, yelling at him to "Get back out there, make that buck, make 'em squirm, make something out of yourself."

A surprise spurt of anger made him mumble, "Make *what*?"

He looked up from those perfect lawyer fingernails just in time. They were rumbling past the cemetery already. At the fifth tree beyond the graveyard's gate, the tallest oak among the dozens spread out among the headstones shot up and demanded its salute: That was Dad. Or at least the tree stood close enough to his father's plot to have become a symbol for the man himself. Every time Frank passed this somber stretch of rail, he felt compelled to tip his hat or cross himself.

If it had been up to him, Frank would have selected a resting place more lush and further beyond the city limits. But the old man wanted to lie down next to his wife, his parents, and his grandparents. This afternoon, however, Frank's anger said the old guy just wanted to keep an eye on things, like the guard at a military base making sure his son didn't go AWOL.

Oooh. Where was this rage coming from?

Frank wasn't sure, but it felt good somehow, necessary somehow. Anger seemed to be the only force strong enough to still the hobnailed boots of guilt doing bloody damage to his ego. *Something* had to silence the internal shriek of condemnation. *Something* had to boost him past the quiet shame of letting the old guy down. Frank's was not a failure of performance, but a derailment of will. He simply didn't want to be the man his father had struggled to make him. It was not that he couldn't cut it. The truth was he longed to try something altogether different, something as far away as possible from Lutterman, Redding and Cole.

Frank Wolf was not the Killer Litigator. Frank Wolf was just a lonely guy on the serious side of forty with a gigantic nest egg but no nest. He was tired and a little confused and far happier tuning up a car engine for a humble wage than he'd ever been making thousands frightening corporate giants on the witness stand. He was a kid-turned-adult, haunted by a frustrated gas station owner reaching out from the grave to kick his son one more rung up a ladder the old man could never have climbed himself. Frank had seized the first opportunity life presented him to back off the front line of super achievement and simply *live*.

He pulled his tie off and buried it inside his briefcase.

"Sorry, Pop," he said, feeling like he owed his father an apology. Maybe his dad owed him one, too.

As the tree and the cemetery slid back behind the train, Frank found himself thinking about a woman whose transmission he had overhauled last week. She had a scruffy eight-year-old boy with her when the minivan limped in, but she wore no wedding ring. A tilted halo of harried courage hung over her dark brown hair and blue eyes. He'd seen that halo before, of course, and had always avoided women who wore it like the plague.

The minivan-mom was supposed to bring it back in for a check-up this week, but Frank figured she'd probably blow off the appointment if the van was running right. Wolf's Auto was his now, though, and he had a reputation for reliability and good customer service to build.

He'd give her a call when he got back to the shop.

DARE I LIVE A HAPPIER LIFE
THAN MY PARENTS?
Brenda's Story

"Are you okay?" her best friend wanted to know.

"What happened?" Brenda asked the blonde cloud floating above her.

"You fainted."

"Oh," said Brenda, as her friend's face came into focus. "Wow." Gradually, the blur hovering behind her maid of honor sharpened its edges, and Brenda recognized the oversized reading glasses riding the dressmaker's nose. Just above those thick lenses, the designer's eyes looked more worried about the wedding dress Brenda had crushed in her swoon than she was concerned about yet another over-anxious bride-to-be.

"Are you okay?" her friend asked again.

"She's fine," the dressmaker said, helping Brenda to her feet. "She's not the first bride to faint in here. You make her eat, make her sleep, she'll be fine."

"I can't make her eat," said Brenda's friend. "She's afraid she won't fit into that dang dress."

"It fit fine two weeks ago, now I need to take it in."

While her maid of honor and dressmaker argued over whether Brenda's low appetite was vanity-in-overdrive or stress-induced, the bride-to-be reached around behind her shoulder blades and set herself free from the gown without their help. She stepped out of the dress and began pulling on her clothes.

"It's a gorgeous dress, Madame Lee," she said, finally coming between the two of them. "I'm sorry about fainting like that. I've never, I mean, I don't know why…"

The designer's face softened. She gathered up her creation and placed a gentle hand on Brenda's arm. "All you brides worry too much. You have friends to worry for you," she said, with a glance at Brenda's companion. "You lean on them. Get the rest you need."

"Did you hear her?" the maid of honor said, climbing into the passenger's seat of Brenda's Jeep. "She practically blamed your fainting on me."

"She said I need more rest, that's all."

"She practically said I wasn't being a good friend!"

"What does she know?" Brenda said, starting the car.

"Listen," said the maid of honor. "Before we go by the florist's, you think we could drive over to Main? I promised Jason I'd pick up his dry-cleaning."

Two hours later, when they had finished running all of the maid of honor's errands, Brenda dropped her friend off at home, insisting that she could handle the floral duty alone. But the florist did not see Brenda at all that afternoon, because the bride-to-be had decided to call the wedding off.

Not only was she exhausted and stressed from trying to handle the wedding details without a reliable friend or her mother and father to lean on, but Brenda suddenly felt buried under an avalanche of doubts about her fiancé's readiness for this step and her own ability to amend her bachelorette ways at the ripe old age of thirty-nine. She found herself stuffed with questions about the authenticity of her love for him and his love for her.

Fainting at the dressmaker's had been an omen, and it wasn't the only one the overcast day would bring either. Even the traffic signals seemed to warn Brenda off the marriage: Every last one was either yellow or red.

She needed to practice telling someone the wedding was off before breaking her man's heart with the bad news, so Brenda steered her Jeep past the city limits and struck out for her Uncle Ray's house. He lived a good two hours' drive away, but she welcomed the uninterrupted hum of the open road and inhaled the bucolic change of scenery. She needed to put some distance between her and all the hopes piled up in not so neat but towering stacks of connubial expectations.

Uncle Ray had always sported a ready-to-soak shoulder. He and his niece had always been particularly close, but that became even more true after Brenda's father died. Ray was the last surviving parental figure in a family devastated by premature exits. Since his brother had checked out of life a year too early to see his little girl tie the knot, Uncle Ray had been delighted Brenda asked him to give her away. He would be very disappointed to hear that the wedding was off, but Brenda knew the maverick in him wouldn't punish her for being true to herself, come what may. He'd understand. After all, he'd never married.

He'll give me one of his squishy, sideways hugs that hurt my shoulder and feel wonderful at the same time, she thought. *He'll ask me if I'm sure. He'll wonder if Jack's done something or said something. He'll think I'm just getting cold feet. But he'll accept it. He'll listen to my reasons, and he'll respect them.*

If only she could remember what those reasons were! As the first foothill grew up out of the valley, the first wave of tears rose up in Brenda's eyes and washed away her rationale for trading in Jack for spinsterhood. By the time she was weaving around the mountains' gentle curves—sneaking glimpses of the lake through the evergreens—she had exhausted her purse's supply of kleenex and had begun using all the left-over fast food napkins. As the Jeep dug its wheels into Ray's steep gravel drive, Brenda reclaimed her doubts about her own readiness for marriage, but all the other issues had washed away like deadwood in a flash flood. She rolled up beside Ray's red truck and was using the sleeve of her sweater to mop up the salty tracks left by the last wave of tears when a huge, bearded face appeared outside her window.

"Hey, there, Pumpkin!" her uncle boomed at her, looking like a slightly domesticated mountain man. He was carrying some firewood and an ax, and his beard was longer than she remembered it. But his smile was pure Ray. "What're you doin' here, and why the hell are you cryin'?"

Brenda rolled down her window. "Hi, Uncle Ray. What's up?"

"I asked you first."

Just as Brenda had expected him to do, Ray listened to her carefully and squished her sideways until it hurt. He got ready to blame

Jack, but then understood this was Brenda's balk, not the groom-to-be's. Ray accepted the disappointment of not getting to perform the traditional bride hand-off without even giving her list of reasons a good poke, which was a relief because the list was very short and rang pretty hollow, even to Brenda. He fed her, and after the meal he poured something warm, sweet and stinging into two snifters. They sipped the liqueur slowly, sitting in front of the fireplace, watching red flames lick the wood Ray fed them. After a long silence, he heaved a sigh and let a soft moan escape through his beard.

"What?" asked Brenda.

"What what?" her uncle smiled.

"What're you thinking?"

He looked at her for a moment as though he weren't certain he should answer. A deep sip from the snifter helped him decide.

"Your dad thought you'd be the one to put an end to the family curse."

"What family curse?"

"You know what curse."

"No, I don't. What are you talking about?"

"Think about it, Pumpkin."

But Brenda didn't want to think about it. She wanted him to make it plain. "What curse, Uncle Ray?"

He took another deep sip and leaned back in his lazy boy, scratching his beard. "Look at me," he said. "What do you see?"

"My favorite uncle hiding under a face blanket."

"Uh-huh. Now look around. What do you see?"

"My uncle. In his…"

"Cave. Alone."

"You could have got married if you wanted, Uncle Ray."

"Oh, at least two or three times."

Brenda grinned at him. "Exactly. You're a loner."

"Really?" he laughed. "Just a free spirit in love with nature and solitude, eh?"

"Well, aren't you?"

Her uncle shrugged. "Guess I damn well better be."

"So, that's supposed to be the big family curse, huh?" Brenda said, setting her glass down. "The whole family's a bunch of commitment phobes, is that it?"

"Well, I'm Grizzly Adams, your big brother's playin' the Wild One with a beer belly jigglin' on his Harley, and you're doin' a Kate Hepburn impersonation."

"Mom and Dad were married for more than thirty years before she died."

"Married for thirty, happy for what? *Five* maybe?"

"I lived with them, Ray, you didn't," Brenda said defensively.

"True. But I got your dad's letters from the frontlines," said Ray. He pushed on in spite of the shock on Brenda's face. "You've had enough therapy by now to tell fact from fantasy, Pumpkin. Don't lie to yourself about what you saw."

Brenda got up and looked out the picture window. The valley she'd crossed to reach him stretched out beyond the tops of fir trees. Her man was down there somewhere, wondering where she was, why she was late for their dinner date. They were supposed to cross the t's and dot the i's on their vows tonight.

"I didn't know your mother's people," her uncle was saying, "but me and your dad, we didn't pop out of some Norman Rockwell fantasy of the perfect family, that's for sure. But so what if your parents didn't do much better? Look at you. Look at this wonderful life you're living. You've got a great career. You own your own house. You make more money than your dad and me put together ever did. You're a beautiful, warm woman with a great sense of humor, and from what your dad told me, this Pete kid isn't the first decent guy to pop the question. Nothin' you've told me today says you don't love him."

"I do."

"Then stand up and say that in front of God and a church full of witnesses!"

Brenda kept her eyes on the view, but she could hear the tears climbing up the back of her uncle's throat. "C'mon, Brenda," he said, "you're pushin' forty. You wanna try tyin' the knot with somebody when you're *fifty* and psychological rigor mortis has set in?"

"So, you think I'm backing out because I'm afraid I'll end up like…"

"Like the rest of us? No, darlin'. I think you're afraid you *won't*. I think you're afraid you'll leave your mom and dad, God rest their sweet but miserable souls, your brother and dear old fuzzy face Ray here in the dust—while you blast off on your merry way, givin' happiness a real run for its money."

He lifted his glass to Brenda in a toast and drank the snifter dry. "Fear of happiness, Pumpkin, that's the family curse," he said. "Wanna try and break it?"

Meditations

Sometimes this picture flashes through my mind: A huge throng (is it the entire six billion inhabitants of Earth?) is processing in lockstep toward a cliff. There is no drum roll, for my imagination runs silent, but the people continue with an inevitable, stoic precision to the edge, dropping like doughnuts at the end of a conveyor belt. Each row of the huge crowd is a generation, and as each peels over the precipice the next moves one step closer. (This image goes way back for me. When I read Catcher in the Rye, *I know what Holden Caulfield was trying to do. He was trying to catch at least one of the "dropees.")*

We all go over that cliff eventually—some of us get there sooner, some later, but all of us get there. That is the way it is. When we lose our parents, we understand that we are that much closer to "NEXT!"

Delle, Frank and Brenda realize this. Delle, as you might have guessed, is the same Delle Chatman who wrote this book, and I am her pastor. The death of Delle's parents set her imagination reeling, providing spools of stories. She has shared them with us because she is a born storyteller and because she believes that this pilgrimage to the precipice should be filled with talk and laughter, shared joy and sorrow. Her warmth and wisdom touch the people she knows and the stories she tells.

In my imagination, I see Holden Caulfield catching some folks as they fall over the cliff. I also see Delle Chatman telling the stories of each one of us as we go to God.

WK

The Eternal
Perspective

The death of a loved one rubs our nose in what we believe about eternal life. No matter how long we've wrestled with our beliefs, no matter how deep or shallow our faith has run up until that moment—when a parent dies every doubt or conviction we've ever entertained about the afterlife rises up full force and dares us to believe or debunk it all over again. Many atheists believe that our fear of death and our dread of everlasting good-byes are the real motives for religion. On a bad day brimming with grief and longing, their assertion can seem quite sound indeed.

But what perspective on death does faith provide? What realities does it construct upon which we can lean and stand and grow? What does it tell us about the meaning of our parents' lives? What does it tell our children about where their grandparents have gone? What does faith say to those of us who remain behind, awaiting our turn to see, to know and to be known—face to face—by our Creator?

Books have been written by and about people who have experienced near death experiences, and their testimonies have some common ground—a dark tunnel, a bright light, a feeling of well-being, loved ones as guides. But these stories quickly diverge into experiences that have idiosyncratic significance and doctrinal diversity. Christians see Jesus, for example, and Buddhists see Buddha. Some see only a bright light. Many describe a judgment-moment that weighs love and fear in the balance rather than good and evil.

But *near*-death is not true death, is it? So, what of those who have left and *not* come back? Where is Mom? Where is Dad? Isn't that what we really want to know? And when they left this world, did they leave us any clues?

THEIR JOURNEY
Eleanor's Story

The water's clarity and the music it made flowing over the rocks lured Eleanor off the bank with the promise that the crossing would be fun if not easy. The day was full of sun, breezy and fresh. The other hikers were a gung-ho bunch who seemed as inexperienced as Eleanor but were wading into the stream eagerly, following the guides without much trepidation. Laughter and satisfied sighs rose into the air above them like butterflies on the wind. Up until now, Eleanor had felt exhausted by the first leg of the trek, which had been all uphill and made her body ache all over. But the gentle chill and the swirl of water around her feet and ankles refreshed and renewed her.

She was thigh-deep in the stream before she even considered the current's strength. It grew more intense as the water deepened, and Eleanor began to have doubts about taking this particular path across the stream. As her guide waded on ahead of her, Eleanor turned to face the bank she'd just left and spied her shoes—all pretty and blue—resting together on the grass where she'd left them. Why on earth had she done that? Whatever made her think she wouldn't need them on the other side?

"Give me your hand, Ellie," said a voice out of the sunshine.

Eleanor looked up, and the guide's perfectly tanned face appeared upside down over her head, framed in sunlight with the branches and leaves of trees providing a windblown halo. He was behind her actually, standing on a boulder she hadn't noticed before. "No turning back now," he said, holding his hand out to her.

Eleanor turned around and let him help her up onto the boulder beside him.

"What were you looking at anyway?" he asked.

"My shoes," Eleanor said, squinting hard to make them out in the tall grass that had sprung up around them in a moment's time. "I didn't want to get them wet."

"They're awfully pretty," said the guide, "but you sure don't need 'em."

"I could've put them in my backpack, if I'd been thinking. Or carried them."

"You'll need both your hands free."

"My daughter bought them for me. I didn't want to spend the money, you know, on shoes I could only wear with one dress."

"They do seem to be quite a special shade of blue," he said, turning round to continue the crossing.

"So was the gown," Eleanor said to his back. "I made it myself. For my fiftieth wedding anniversary."

"Your *fiftieth*? My goodness, what a glorious accomplishment!" He took a short step to a smaller boulder, but there was room enough for both of them on it. "This next chunk's a little tricky. Just step where I step…and stay close, all right?"

Eleanor nodded, but she kept talking to keep her mind off their high-wire act. "You don't see many marriages lasting half a century, you know."

"Sad but true," he said, leading her over a chain of rocks just big enough to use as steppingstones, one at a time. "You made the dress yourself, you say?"

"I made most of the kids' clothes when they were growing up," Eleanor recalled with pride. "Then I even sewed some of the grand-kids' clothes when they were little before everything had to have some designer label on it. Hardest part about the dress was getting these gnarly, old hands of mine to agree to it."

"Well, I think you *deserved* some pretty blue shoes," said the guide, stepping up onto the next large boulder sitting midstream. He pulled her up beside him, and then they sat down to give her a little rest.

"The point is, Betty couldn't afford those shoes any more than I could," said Eleanor, "and if she keeps spending like that…"

"She won't. She's got a good head on her shoulders, Ellie. She'll figure it out. The hard way maybe, over time. But eventually, she'll learn."

Eleanor wasn't so sure. Her daughter and son had both taken after their poor departed father, who had never been able to resist chasing after whatever his dreamer's heart desired.

"My husband must have launched a new career every ten years, invested in three or four go-nowhere businesses," she said. "A sweetheart, a decent provider by the skin of his teeth, my Bill. But he fed our kids some wild fantasies."

"Blue shoe fantasies," the guide smiled.

"I was the pragmatist of the bunch," Eleanor insisted.

"Somebody had to be."

"Exactly. The rest of them had their heads in the clouds all the time. One of us had to keep her feet on the ground."

"One of us had to," he echoed, getting back on his feet.

"I know they're not kids anymore. They're grown up, with families of their own, but..."

"What are they going to do without you?"

Eleanor stood up, too, her eyes on the shore she'd left behind. A forest had swallowed the tall grass, and with it her blue shoes.

In fact, the bank she'd left behind just minutes before seemed totally altered.

"Yes," she said, "what are they going to do without me?"

"Who says they're without you?" the guide sang back at her over his shoulder as he moved along another chain of stones toward the other shore.

"It's pretty obvious, isn't it?" Eleanor said, hurrying to follow him. "I'm here with you and not there with them, aren't I?"

"Well, actually, you're both," he said, hopping onto the last and tallest boulder. There was nothing but rushing water between that rock and the bank.

"That doesn't make sense," the pragmatist in Eleanor declared as he tugged her up beside him once more. "How can I be here and there at the same time?"

"Well, that's an excellent question, Ellie. Let me see if I can give you a decent answer." He took off his cap, wiped the thin film of perspiration from his brow, and then studied the hat's insides thoughtfully, as if he expected the wisdom of the ages to be buried inside its brim. Eleanor vaguely remembered someone else who used to do that: pull his best lines out of a baseball cap.

"Not so long ago," he said finally, "a wise little girl took me across this stream, or a stream like it anyway, and she said that when you die your spirit goes but your love stays. That's how you can be here with me and there with them."

"A little girl, huh?"

He put the cap on again and turned back to the task at hand. Clearly, they had to climb back down into the river's current in order to finish crossing over. "Maybe you better let me have that," he said, slipping the knapsack off Eleanor's back. "I should've taken it off your back before now really."

Suddenly, she felt light enough to float away on the next breeze. "Better, huh?"

"*Worlds* better," Eleanor admitted. "I always over-pack."

"You certainly do," he said, testing the knapsack's weight in his hands. "Not a problem," he said with a smile, and launched her backpack downstream on the river's swirling current.

Eleanor's mouth fell open. She watched hikers and guides below them dodge her pack as it drifted by. Not one of them even tried to catch it for her. For the first time, she noticed hers was not the only luggage gliding out of sight.

"Why did you do that?" she demanded. "That was mine."

"Yep," the guide said cheerfully, "but I bet you can't tell me what was in it."

He was right. She couldn't remember a single thing she'd tucked away, even though she'd checked that knapsack over and over before setting out on her journey. Nevertheless, Eleanor McHenry was not used to being out of control. Nor was she accustomed to someone having more answers than she or telling her she was better off without this or that or making her feel as if her children did not need her anymore. "I didn't say they don't need you," the guide said, able to discern her thoughts without hearing them. "Maybe it's time your children learned to lean on someone else, the way you learned to lean on a Stronger Arm when their father died."

He slid off the boulder and carefully felt for the best footing on the riverbed. The water came up to his chest. He reached for Eleanor with both hands. When she slid down into his arms, he held her closer than he had before and lowered her gently into the stream.

As soon as her feet settled firmly on the bottom—smooth like velvet sand on a virgin beach—Eleanor could see that the stream swirling around them was no longer coursing water but a current of clouds as soft and white as those she had seen blowing overhead on that perfect spring day half a century ago when she had married her husband, Bill.

And at last she could see that this perfectly tanned young man was that same dream spinner, her best friend and life partner found again after five decades of marriage, five years of widowhood, and Eleanor's own long, hard battle with death.

"Good to see you, Ellie," Bill said. "How are you, honey?"

"Fine now," she said, and rested her head on his shoulder for awhile.

"Still got a ways to go," he told her.

"I know," she said.

As their legs pushed toward the other shore, clouds sailed between them, bathed in a sunlight that grew warmer and brighter with every step.

He released her, though, just as they reached the edge of Time. He took a step back so he could follow rather than lead. Eleanor started to ask why, but realized she already knew the answer: One by one, each soul steps into glory. He had made his grand entrance long ago. This moment was all hers.

"Who's the dreamer now?" her husband asked the old lady Eleanor once was, for her body had grown as young and strong as his own.

Her smile was answer enough.

When Eleanor McHenry slipped into Eternity, her bare feet rode the tail of a comet, while galaxies combed her hair.

Meditation

One time I took a pilgrimage to the Holy Land with forty-five of my parishioners. We prepared for our journey by extensive study together and developed a real sense of connection with one another even before we left. The result was a blissful two weeks in Israel.

In a similar fashion, some parishioners and I recently prepared together for the inevitable "pilgrimage of death." that is part of the human condition. Led by one of our members, a retired lay theologian, we thought about the subject in new ways, shared our doubts and fears, weighed various theories about the hereafter, and discussed our deepest hopes and fondest dreams. Our tales were as rich as Canterbury's, our detours as interesting as the main road. Nothing could have been less macabre or more stimulating. We all concluded that we do not really know anything for certain about life after death, but that realization seemed to satisfy rather than disturb us.

We did, however, change the way we imagined death and beyond, and Eleanor's story is an example of how to do that. It helps us form new images, opens us to further insight and understanding. So it is that we become part of the storytelling along the way: We hear Eleanor's story, then we tell our own. It is in the telling and the hearing that the pilgrimage of life is made.

It is said that God made us because He loves stories.

WK

Conclusion
The Legacy of Faith

During the cold winter months of her kindergarten year, my daughter delighted in pulling her hat down over her face to keep the chill off her cheeks. She would yank the hat down over her eyes with one hand, thrust the other into mine, and giggle for an entire city block as I led her down the sidewalk, dodging patches of ice and the occasional pedestrian. Depending on how rushed we were to arrive on time, I either tolerated the game or ended it by insisting she self-navigate so we could make better time. But I always marveled at the total faith she had in my ability to keep her from walking where she shouldn't and to hold all trouble at bay. I knew she would never give anyone else this much control or power over her—and most often I don't want her to give it to me.

I was raised by parents who made certain that I learned the tenets of the Catholic faith. In my early days, they rehearsed my catechism lessons, and until my senior year in high school they made certain I attended Mass, went to catechism classes, and observed the holy days of obligation. They were particularly insistent that I obeyed the fourth commandment and always told them the truth.

Decades later, when my life was fully my own to do with as I pleased, I did just that, until heartbreak and disturbing trials blew frost across my cheeks. Eventually, I realized I was suffering from self-inflicted blindness and definitely had no reliable hand to hold. I hunted feverishly for alternatives to my "parents' religion," until my father's mother paid me a visit one day out of the blue and gave me a Bible. She told me that within its covers I might reunite with Someone I already knew, Someone far wiser and far more available than even my Mom and Dad.

I've lived another twenty years since that day, and now all of those life pillars—mother, father, grandmother– one by one have gone on to glory. Those hands I trusted, like my daughter now trusts mine, all had to let mine go.

And yet, my hands are not empty.

I am not without deep companionship and loving guidance.

Nor am I without a palpable bond with those who loved me into life.

I've inherited a great deal from my parents—much of their strengths, some of their weaknesses, most of their talents, and a portion of their courage. But the single, most precious legacy I have inherited was pressed into my consciousness the moment each of them passed away. It is the same precious legacy I will attempt to pass on to the little girl who likes to walk blindfolded to school, her hand in mine.

The faith of our fathers and mothers may have been strong or weak. It may have been lived out fully or shunted to the periphery of their daily lives. As their children, we may have accepted or rejected it or allowed it to languish lukewarm and undernourished. Their deaths are often the most profound test of what we ourselves believe about God, about ourselves, about life, about the hereafter.

It is my hope that these stories and the meditations by Father Kenneally have ushered you a little deeper into the mysterious workings of your own heart and soul. I pray that these fictitious folk I've created—who have endured some make-believe sliver of the real loss you and I know—miraculously help you realize that many, many others have traveled this same rugged territory.

None of us ever has to walk through our valleys alone.

Acknowledgements

When they learned I was writing a book about the loss of a parent, many friends and acquaintances shared their personal experiences with me. Though I spun this book's tapestry out of fiction rather than fact, I'm indebted to each and every one of them for that gift of empathy and trust.

I give thanks for my extended family, all of whom help keep my torch lit: the McDaniels in Kansas City, Missouri and Happy Bend, Arkansas; my dear Aunt Lossie Sellers; my grandmother Delphine McClain (rest in peace); my "play mothers" Etta Ellis and Martha Meriwether; my creative backstops Pamela Sherrod, Jane Lawrence, Christopher Derfler and Anita Fitch; my back-up mom Mae Morris; my fellow parishioners at St. Gertrude's Catholic Church; and all the friends who have supported me with their wisdom, prayers and love. A deep thanks goes out to Christian authors Frances J. Roberts and Joan Sturkie for their friendship, example and encouragement.

To Grace McCann and Lavern Chatman, God bless you for helping our parents through and over.

I'm particularly grateful to my brother Christopher for letting me try these stories out on him—sometimes in the middle of the night; to my brother Gregory for his unflinching confidence in my ability to heal people through my art; and to our big brother Jim for showing us how faithfully guardian angels keep watch over us when our parents no longer can.

And a "first hug of the day" to my daughter, Ramona.

Thanks for the inspiration and your patience.

Other Grief Resources

The Death of a Wife: Reflections for a Grieving Husband by Robert L. Vogt. A collection of poignant reflections for any husband mourning the death of his wife. Each of the thirty-one brief stories, remembrances, meditations and poems considers a different facet of the grieving process for men. (112 pages, $9.95)

The Death of a Husband: Reflections for a Grieving Wife by Helen Reichert Lambin. Over forty reflections for any wife mourning the death of her husband offer insights that will touch a woman's heart, heal her soul, and point out new and hopeful directions for her life. (128 pages, $9.95)

The Death of a Child: Reflections for Grieving Parents by Elaine E. Stillwell. Filled with examples of people who have lost a child and how they dealt with the reality of that event. This collection of life-giving lessons touches on the wide range of emotions and situations that parents encounter after the death of their child. (160 pages, $9.95)

The New Day Journal: A Journey from Grief to Healing by Sr. Mauryeen O'Brien. Designed to help those mourning the loss of a loved one work their way through the four tasks of grief: accepting the reality of the loss, experiencing the pain of grief, adjusting to change, and creating memories and goals. (96 pages, $9.95)

From Grief to Grace: Images for Overcoming Sadness and Loss by Helen Reichert Lambin. This unique, gentle book addresses the powerful emotions common to all experiences of grief, using images—some religious and some secular—to assist people in naming, processing and overcoming their grief. (96 pages, $8.95)

Hidden Presence: Twelve Blessings That Transformed Sorrow or Loss edited by Gregory F. Augustine Pierce. Real stories by twelve spiritual writers about a tragedy they experienced that led to a real blessing in their lives. (176 pages, hardcover with gift ribbon, $17.95)

Available from booksellers or call (800) 397-2282
www.actapublications.com